T0171567

BREAKING THE CHAINS
OF
SPIRITUAL BONDAGE
BETWEEN
MAN AND GODS CREATURES

REBECCA ANN NORMANDIN

WestBow
PRESS
A DIVISION OF THOMAS NELSON

WestBow Press books may be ordered through booksellers or by contacting:

WestBow Press
A Division of Thomas Nelson
1663 Liberty Drive
Bloomington, IN 47403
www.westbowpress.com
1-(866) 928-1240

ISBN: 978-1-4497-2910-3 (sc)
ISBN: 978-1-4497-2909-7 (e)

Library of Congress Control Number: 2011918268

Printed in the United States of America

WestBow Press rev. date: 02/22/2012

DEDICATION

I have only one person to thank for all the blessings in my life and for inspiring me to write this book. He is my Lord and Savior, Jesus Christ of Nazareth.

CONTENTS

INTRODUCTION

J ust like the Word of God is for mankind, so it is for all the animals of
this earth. I was just a teenager when I finally saw it. I finally received
this revelation from Jehovah God that He had been showing me all my
life, it dropped into my heart. For some reason, I guess I had been looking
through my religious goggles and I just didn't see it. I thought that the
Bible was only for people, not for animals. After all, we are human, and
they're not. This revelation that God showed me turned my whole view of
the world concerning the Bible and animals upside down.

God showed me the spiritual chains, yokes, and bondages that can be
erected in people's lives when they do not correctly care for the animals
they own or are entrusted to care for. The Garden of Eden is God's
blueprint to us on how He expects animals to be cared for until they are
all raptured up to heaven with all who have accepted Jesus as their King
and Savior.

And have you ever wondered what Sasquatch, Bigfoot, Skunk apes,
Yeti's, The Abominable Snowman, and yes even the Loch ness Monster
are and where did they ever come from in the first place? They are not
a myth. They are very, very real and very, very dangerous. They are not
what you thought they were. I will take you through the Bible where it
reveals exactly what they really are and where they came from. Now for
the first time you will know what they really are and how they came to
be on this earth.

These truths have been starring us right in our faces ever since the
Garden of Eden, and now I will point them out to you causing the veil to

be pulled back just a little more in this area. Now the veil between man and the spirit realm cannot be fully removed, because a mere mortal could not withstand seeing the spirit realm completely. This is recorded throughout the Bible when an angel of the Lord revealed itself to a man. Many times men were so gripped with fear that they fell to the ground motionless.

Hopefully now we all can see a little clearer what it is that God has been trying to show us all along. So fasten your spiritual seatbelts, because you're about to fall off that religious chair of yours. Get ready to have those cobwebs of bad teachings and handed-down traditions blasted right out of your mind. I'm not kidding you; it's time for all of us to wake up, so hold on, because you're in for a bumpy ride. God expects us to respect the life of each and every animal up to the moment of its death. That also means for us to provide an excellent life for the animal in our care and a pain-free death if at all possible.

Acknowledgments

First and foremost, I give my deepest thanks and acknowledgment to Jesus Christ of Nazareth. If it were not for His Word, I would still be in darkness blind to the truth. And I would also like to thank two of my mentors and teachers, Drs. Jack and Rexella Van Impe, for having the courage to not beat around the bush and to really preach the unperverted Word of Jesus Christ of Nazareth. So many times I would be watching another minister preach and I found myself telling the preacher, "Please, please, just come out and say it, for gosh sakes, and stop being so vague." Not you, Dr. Van Impe. You are not one of those cowards trying to stay neutral. You come out and say it just like Jesus did. Whenever you introduce a new DVD, you always give credit to our fathers of Christendom and all of your other resources that you used in your research on your show *Jack Van Impe Presents*. Here are just some of Dr. Van Impe's teachings on DVD and VHS that were used in the research of this book. I watched some no less than fifteen to thirty times each, if only to learn the truth.

1. *The Truth About Heaven* (DVD)
2. *Beyond the Grave* (VHS)
3. *Angels and Demons* (DVD)
4. *Animals in Heaven* (DVD)
5. *The Final Seven Signs* (DVD)
6. *Addictions* (DVD)
7. *The Big Ten: Religious Delusions, Distortions, and Deceptions* (DVD)
8. *Attack on Christian America: The UN's Threat to Your Beliefs* (DVD)

9. *Reclaiming and Restoring Biblical Christianity* (DVD)
10. *Dictator of the New World Order: Alive and Waiting in the Wings* (DVD)
11. *New World Order Rising* (DVD)
12. *11:59: The Countdown* (DVD)
13. *The Rapture:* (DVD)
14. *Global ID: 666* (DVD)
15. *December 21, 2012: History's Final Day?* (DVD)
16. *Christ Returns: This Generation?* (DVD)
17. *Day Eight: Planet Earth Forever* (VHS)

I also want to acknowledge Dr. Perry Stone from his T.V. show *Manna-fest* for his many hours of in-depth research and teachings. Here are some of his teachings on DVD. I want to give credit where credit is due. I also researched these DVDs no less than fifteen to thirty times each from beginning to end.

1. *Fallen Angels, Giants, and Evil Spirits* (DVD)
2. *Unlocking the Millennial Code* (DVD)
3. *Purging Your House* (DVD)

And last, but not least, I want to acknowledge Dr. Carl Baugh and his Creation Evidence Museum in Texas. Dr. Baugh has kept true to the Word of God in his research that clearly reveals that Jehovah God, the Holy Spirit, and Jesus Christ of Nazareth, the Trinity, are the Creators of the universe. I want everyone to know that I do not just listen to a handful of teachers, preachers or evangelists. What I do is I listen to every man and woman of God that the Holy Spirit guides me into learning from. I will get all their tapes, books and D.V.D.'s. I have done this since I was a teenager which makes-up quite a large span of ministers.

CHAPTER 1

OBEDIENT TO THE VOICE OF GOD

J ust let me say that when the Holy Spirit talks to you, you had better listen and do what He is telling you to do. After all, it's for your good.

The first type of animal that I was ever introduced to was dogs. My Grandfather Ferguson loved raccoon hunting in Indiana, and he had a couple of hounds. My mother and I lived with Grandpa and Grandma Ferguson for three and a half wonderful years. My mother divorced my father when I was one year old; that was in 1961. My mother was the only girl out of eight boys, four younger than her and four older than her. Her four younger brothers were still living at home. Of course, I was Grandpa's little princess, and with all my uncles spoiling me—well, you get the picture.

I loved to go and feed one of my grandfather's hounds, a black-and-tan named Rowdy, through the wire of his pen out in the backyard. Onetime one of my younger uncles snuck up behind me while I was sharing my peanut butter and jelly sandwich with Rowdy. My uncle Tony picked me up into the air and then put me back down on the ground. Then he pretended that he was hurting me, just to infuriate Rowdy, and it did. I pulled away from my uncle laughing and giggling and ran straight back to Rowdy. He licked my hands and smelled me to make sure that I was all right; it was all just in fun.

Then, about a year later, my grandfather came home from hunting one night. I was peering around the corner from another room listening to Grandfather's voice as he told everyone sitting around the kitchen table that he had found Rowdy dead on a road. My heart felt like it was going to burst, and my eyes welled up with tears. My best friend was dead. Rowdy was what hunters' called a silencer; it means that they are silent while on the trail. They don't start to howl and bay until they have treed the raccoon. My grandfather said that he and his hunting buddies thought that the raccoon that Rowdy had picked the scent up on had crossed a busy road and ran into the forest to the other side, and of course Rowdy followed. He was an excellent tracker. Grandfather said that he and his friends searched all night long for Rowdy. He was Grandpa's favorite.

Can you imagine the horrible feelings inside everyone's stomachs as they called and called for him for hours? Then their fears finally came true. There he layout on a cold, black road. Rowdy's body was only visible by the bright moonlight. My grandfather said whoever hit him just kept on driving. I still haven't forgotten my childhood friend Rowdy. Thank God I'll see him and all my other pets again in heaven. I believe that all animals will be resurrected to live in the renewed heaven and the renewed earth.

As much as I loved my grandfather, there were things I saw him do that I didn't like, even as a three- and four-year-old, such as the way I saw him load the dogs up into the trunk of his car to go hunting for raccoons. It wasn't until I got older that I began to verbalize my anger about how people treat their animals.

I can remember when I was five years old in El Paso, Texas. I was walking down the sidewalk a couple of doors down from my house; it was much safer back then. I can remember as I passed every house, I could see a dog tied in its own yard on a chain at each house. Even at this young age, in my eyes and inside my spirit I knew this was wrong. The Holy Spirit fell upon me and first started talking to me about these dogs who were barking at me from across the street. I just stood their motionless starring at those dogs and listening to the voice of the Lord. He said that *"These dogs were not supposed to be on chains and left outside in weather that we humans could not even endure ourselves"*. What I saw that day and heard the Holy Spirit say to me I will never forget. Or all the other countless

2

times throughout my life growing up. Whenever The Holy Spirit spoke to me about this subject concerning the animals of the earth He would say *"Don't forget that,* or that, or that". It was like I would hear this kind of ping sound and the Holy spirit would magnifier that memory. And He would always say *"Don't forget that"*. I knew that He was using all of what I saw to teach me something at a later date. And now I know that it was all done to put into this book.

I receive emails each morning from Pastor Mike Murdock from WisdomOnline.com called Morning Motivations. I want you to read what one of Dr. Murdock's inspirational messages was that I believe to be true. It is titled, *"Discern Your Assignment."*

When God created you, He gave you certain gifts and talents to accomplish something he wanted you to do. We call that an "assignment." *The problem that infuriates you the most is often the problem God has assigned you to solve.* Everything God creates is a solution to something. You are a life-jacket to someone drowning. Find them. *Those who unlock your compassion are those to whom you have been assigned. "I will praise Thee; for I am fearfully and wonderfully made: marvelous are Thy works; and that my soul knoweth right well."*

That's why I'm writing this book. I felt God's pain and sorrow as I looked at those dogs across the street in El Paso, and I still feel His pain. I believe that is why this subject has always bothered me and gnawed at me, even to this day. You can have more than one assignment. I know without a shadow of a doubt that I have two assignments. The first assignment is to evangelize the world and to pull as many people as possible out of Satan's hold and into the kingdom of God. I remember when I was in total darkness, and it makes me spitting mad when I meet people who just do not know the truth, the Good News, the Bible. My second assignment is to help the animals of this earth who are owned by someone to live and be cared for the way Jehovah God intended for them to live and be cared for.

My prayer is that this book will help animals to stop getting the short end of the proverbial stick, which from my observation happens 90 percent of the time. And for all those animal lovers out there who don't know Jesus of Nazareth or His Word. I pray that after reading this book. That you will finally know Him and His Word. To know the real Him not what liars say about Him or His Word. I also realize that for some of you this may be the first time you have ever read Him. Because reading His Word is meeting Jesus of Nazareth. Don't be afraid this is what you have been searching for all of your life, it is in this book.

The first memory that I have of my parents taking me to Sunday school was as a small child of four years of age to learn about Jesus. As I sometimes sat in church looking up at them, I got the distinct feeling that they only did it because they thought the socially right thing to do in 1964 was to bring your children to church; I truly don't believe that they wanted to go themselves, but I am very thankful that they did. At the age of eight, I fell in love with Jesus so much so that I wanted to go into ministry so that I could serve Him forever, but in 1968, the only women I knew in ministry were nuns. As I grew up into my teens, I accepted Jesus as my King and Savior, and I continued to grow up spiritually throughout my twenties and on into my thirties. The Holy Spirit's voice just kept getting louder and more dominant. I'm so embarrassed to say it, but I have to confess that I didn't start to write this book until 1999. And at that point in time I had over ninety percent of it written. I was thirty-nine years of age then. The Holy Spirit added Chapter Eight a couple of months before the book was published in 2011 along with a couple of other nuggets of revelation. The truth of the matter is that The Holy Spirit dictated to me 95% of the book and only 10% is me. I just typed, thank you Lord! This book has been germinating inside of my spirit ever since I was four years old. I just never had the courage or the strength before to go and write it.

Well here I am. It's Labor day, and this baby's coming out. The Holy Spirit has been doing somersaults inside of me all my life trying to get this out of me, and now I can't keep quiet anymore. When I first started writing, I poured out all of my anger at how bad I'd seen people treat animals. I saw four out of five families or people who had just gotten a new puppy give it up in two or three months. Out into the backyard that baby went; it never failed.

Then, after a month of writing and getting out all my complaints about all the times I heard or saw animals being mistreated, something changed. I felt the strong presence of the Holy Spirit on me and around me it was inside the whole room. It was His anointing. Then the Holy Spirit spoke to my spirit and told me to erase the name that I had previously called this book. It happened so fast, and He was so definite about what the title should be. I didn't have time to not believe what I heard. I immediately heard myself say. "But I like the title that I named it. And then again the Holy Spirit said in a strong tone. *"Change the name you're naming it, Breaking The Chains Of Spiritual Bondage Between Man And God's Creatures."* So I deleted the name that I had named it first and replaced it with the title that the Holy Spirit told me to name it. I let out a sigh and leaned back in my chair and said, "Wow!"

I did as the Lord instructed me. From that moment on, I found that it was not me but the Spirit of God speaking to my spirit. I would just type what God told me to write. The point I'm trying to make here is that these are not my words, and this is not my book. These are God's words, and this is His book, and He wants the whole world to receive what He has to say. Now I know why my heart has been so tender toward animals all my life. I've noticed that the more spiritually mature that I get, the more outspoken I am when I see animal cruelty. I will speak up instead of being quiet.

It's as if the Holy Spirit that lives inside of me wants to tell the whole world. *"Stop hurting my animals."* God is saying to us. *"My nature is love, and I will not bless cruelty or neglect".* God created man in His image, and living inside of every born-again, Spirit-filled Christian is His nature which is love, mercy and kindness. In the past I've seen again and again people who know little or nothing about animals or how to care for them owning them. This has to stop. I believe that our laws need to be updated. The cruelty that is now only considered as a misdemeanor should be upgraded as a felony. It's just too crazy and dangerous for the authorities to allow an animal to be in the care of an ignorant or cruel owner. We should not be giving an animal to just anybody. They must prove that they are knowledgeable and worthy to own this animal. If you own any animal, it's your responsibility to teach your pet words just like you would teach any human child words and the objects that go with each word. In the Garden of Eden animals spoke i.e. the snake that talked to Eve in the Garden of Eden. And in the new age on the eight day when the animals are all brought back to re-populate the renewed earth, they will speak again.

Just start teaching your pet as young as possible, but if you have an older animal, don't worry, you can teach them also. It's done by repetition, patience, and love. Always stick with the same word with the same object. This is so your animal can communicate to you all of its wants, needs, and desires. Are you stunned? You didn't know that animals have wants, needs, and desires. Well hang onto your pants because they do, and there are a lot of them. Animals that are not living in the wild but living with you are high maintenance. They are a lot of work. It's a twenty-four-seven labor of love if you're doing it right. For example, if you have two kids, two dogs, and a bird, you now have five kids to feed and provide everything for. And if you own herds such as one hundred head of cattle. You now have one hundred kids, to provide for, mommy and daddy. I'm dead serious. You see if what you just read blows your mind. Then it proves that your thinking does not line up with God's way of thinking. *Luke 12:48* Read in the context of verses 42-48. *"To whom much is given much will be required"*.

If you have cats and you don't have an electric cat box, then the cat box must be cleaned three to four times each day. You're animals see you and your spouse as the alpha male and female and as their parents.

When you're outside, check the ground first with your hand. If it's too hot for your hand, then it's defiantly too hot for your animal's feet. This is also true for hoofed animals such as horses.

When the iron on their hooves heats up from the ground, such as hot asphalt, it's just like walking on a skillet. A horse's hoof is made up of the same thing that your fingernail is made up of, and that is carotene. For more information on the hooves of horse's, you can check out a magazine called *Farrier's Digest*.

Job 12:9–10 says, *"Which of all these does not know that the hand of the Lord has done this? In his hand is, the life of every creature and the breath of all mankind."*

Jehovah God created the universe and He sees all that is done in it nobody gets away with sin here on this earth. With the Garden of Eden, as our example we can clearly deduce that there is a right way and a wrong way to care for the animals that we each are in stewardship over.

Chapter 2

God Created the Heavens and the Earth

I'm a straight forward, just give me the facts, ma'am, type of girl. Personally I want the truth and only the truth. I'm only interested in what Jehovah God has to say about pretty much everything. I want to know His take on the universe He has created. I want to see it through his eyes, and I pray that you do too. With all of my heart, I want you to understand all of this, so of course we have to start where? Yes, at the beginning in Genesis. God's Word will help me to connect the dots sort of speak and you too will see what He has been constantly saying to me about the animals of this earth. Don't cry—by the time you read the last words of this book, you will be jumping for joy.

So many people believe that this earth was created by the big bang or that man and animals slithered out of a pond. Personally, I believe what Jehovah God's Word says. Genesis 1:1 says: *"In the beginning God made the heavens and the earth."* Exodus 20:11 says *"For in six days the Lord made the heavens and the earth, the sea, and everything in them."* Psalm 100:3 says: *"It is he who has made us, and not we."* Genesis 2:18–23 says:

> And the Lord God said, *"It is not good for man to be alone.*
> *I will make a companion who will help him." So the Lord*

God formed from the soil every kind of animal and bird. He brought them to Adam to see what he the livestock, birds, and wild animals. But still there was no companion suitable for him. So the Lord caused Adam to fall into a deep sleep. He took one of Adams ribs and closed up the place from which he had taken it. Then the Lord God made a woman from the rib and brought her to Adam. "At last!" Adam exclaimed. "She is part of my own flesh and bone! She will be called woman, because she was taken out of man."

Genesis 3:1–15 says:

Now, the serpent was the shrewdest of all the creatures the Lord God had made. "Really?" he asked the woman. "Did God really say you must not eat any of the fruit in the garden?" "Of course we may eat it," the woman told him. "It's only the fruit from the tree at the center of the garden that we are not allowed to eat. God says we must not eat it or even touch it, or we will die." "You won't die!" the serpent hissed. "God knows that your eyes will be opened when you eat it. You will become just like God, knowing everything both good and evil." The woman was convinced. The fruit looked so fresh and delicious, and it would make her so wise! So she ate some of the fruit. She also gave some to her husband who was with her. Then he ate it, too. At that moment, their eyes were opened, and they suddenly felt shame at their nakedness. So they strung fig leaves together around their hips to cover themselves. Toward evening they heard the Lord God walking about in the garden, so they hid themselves among the trees. The Lord God called to Adam, "Where are you?" He replied, "I heard you, so I hid. I was afraid because I was naked." "Who told you that you were naked?" the Lord God asked. "Have you eaten the fruit I commanded you not to eat?" "Yes," Adam admitted, "but it was the woman you gave me who brought me the fruit, and I ate it." Then the

*Lord asked the woman, "How could you do such a thing?"
"The serpent tricked me," she replied. "That's why I ate it."
So the Lord God said to the serpent, "Because you have done
this, you will be punished. You are singled out from all the
domestic and wild animals of the whole earth to be cursed.
You will grovel in the dust as long as you live, crawling along
on your belly. From now on, you and the woman will be
enemies, and your offspring and her offspring will be enemies.
He will crush your head, and you will strike his heel."*

Genesis 2:15 says: "*The Lord placed the man in the garden of Eden to
tend and care for it. But the Lord gave him this warning: 'You may freely eat
any fruit in the garden except fruit from the tree of the knowledge of good and
evil.'*"

God said, "*If you eat of it, on that very day you shall die.*" God didn't
mean that they would physically drop dead that very moment. God meant
their immortality would cease that very moment and their bodies would
become mortal that very moment. Now because of that sin the bodies of
man and animals die little by little every moment of every day. Before
their sinful act, all of the animal's bodies and Adam and Eve's bodies
were imperishable, meaning that they would never die. Adam and Eve
were **eternal beings** and all the animals were **eternal creatures**. And
now along with the curse this fallen earth that we live in is also attacking
our physical bodies and killing us. It might be very, very slow, but we're
perishing nonetheless. Mainly it's the air that we breathe in this atmosphere
with all its free radicals and noxious poisons that are attacking our now-
mortal bodies. The dangerous climate changes all over the world are only
going to get worse. Eden and the earth now are as different from each other
as the color white is from black and as opposite as light is to dark. I can't
emphasize enough just how large the difference is. Let's imagine that the
Garden of Eden was manifested here on earth in today's time along with
its ultrapure atmosphere and climate. All who entered it would swear that
they were on another planet. In fact, every one of the people's bodies who
entered this Eden would start to heal in that healthy, life-giving air and
atmosphere.

It's contrary to the atmosphere we all live in today, which is choking the life out of us. Your body won't show the effects for decades to come, but it is happening. There are also spiritual attacks to you and to the animals of this earth that you must address.

The devil is an equal-opportunity attacker. As you read through this book, I will be exposing many of the lies that have kept people in deep spiritual bondage. In some cases, people don't even know where to begin to get themselves out of their bondage. I will reveal the sins that cause people to fall into these spiritual "traps, pits, or snares," as the Bible calls them. These will be concerning the animals of this earth, especially the ones that you own and care for. The spirit of your adversary, the devil, doesn't stand in front of you with his hair on fire and say, "Hey, you're sinning with the animals." No, he wants you to stay in these bondages. Have you ever heard that saying, "What you don't know won't hurt you"? Well that's a lie straight from hell. What you don't know will steal from you and kill you, and that's exactly what the devil is hoping for.

We are now in the last years before the saved will be raptured up to the third heaven, out of harm's way, to attend the wedding feast with Jesus. Then, all those who are left behind will go through the seven years of tribulation. At the end of those seven years, Jesus of Nazareth will return with His armies that's us, the raptured. To win the battle against the enemies of Jehovah God at Armageddon. Anyone who has not accepted Jesus Christ as their Lord and savior will drop dead where they stand at that battle. They will all be resurrected again at the end of the thousand year reign to be judged by our Lord Jesus Christ. The one and only true God and Lord of Lords and King of Kings. I don't want to get off track, but briefly, here are seven of the last signs that must happen before Jesus return. Now there was no Israel for 2,534 years until 1948 when Israel became a nation.

Here are seven signs that must come to pass before Christ returns.

1. *Israel must become a nation*
2. *Jerusalem captured by the Jews*
3. *Revival of a new European Union*
4. *Rapture of the believers up to heaven*
5. *A mighty Russia*
6. *A mighty China*
7. *A mighty Iran*

Please do not be mistaken; Jesus is not returning to destroy the earth. He is returning to re-claim His throne in Jerusalem and to set up His eternal kingdom here on earth. During His thousand year reign Heaven will also be re-located to earth. This is at the beginning of His thousand year reign when Jesus Christ will say to all who have accepted Him as their Lord and Savior, "Come in and inherit the earth." God will bring in the greatest harvest of souls into His kingdom during the tribulation. Our Lord Jesus is coming back for a free church, not a bound church. But He doesn't just want His body of believers to be free of every form of spiritual bondage and from oppression and possession of demonic spirits that were released into the earth whenever a giant died. I addressed this in greater detail in chapter 8. He also wants the secular world loosed from the bondage and attacks of these lying spirits and demons. But most of all He wants the secular world all saved, to accept Jesus Christ as Lord of their lives.

People's lack of revelation knowledge in the Bible will inadvertently let these spiritual chains, yokes, bondages, and demons attach themselves to their lives. There are so many different ways that these bondages can be erected in people's lives while demons attach themselves to and possess an individual. Here are just a few that the Holy Spirit has shown me over the years. Sin is sin, whether it's against a human or an animal you need to know this spiritual law. For example, let's say you know of an animal that's not being cared for and you do nothing. Or let's say someone has left an animal on your land or at your home, whatever the reason is. They're gone for a few days or a few weeks, or they just don't come back at all. During this time, in God's eyes, you're responsible for all the needs of that animal.Because you now know about it, you cannot just turn a blind eye and think it's not my animal and do nothing!

Or let's say you're carrying a load of animals to market and the trailer that you are hauling them in is open. Just like you need heat and air conditioning, so do they. I've seen trucks with open compartments carry cattle, pigs, and sometimes chickens down the highway in the winter and also in the suffocating heat of summer. If you're saying in your heart, *"Well it's not my animal; it doesn't belong to me,"* then just think to yourself, *What would Jesus do?* Use the Garden of Eden as your blueprint, and then do it. Until Jesus returns to fix the broken thermostat of this earth's climate back to the seventy-five degrees of the Garden of Eden, we are all in this together. That means yes, we are all responsible for each other and the animals of this earth. For the people who make trailers and barns for animals, here's your financial opportunity to make millions. Start by building all trailers and barns with an air conditioning unit and heating units inside of them. This is so your animals will always be in a seventy-five degree environment. If Jehovah God provided for man and all the animals a seventy-five degree environment to live in forever. The Garden of Eden is our example from Jehovah God as to what temperature man and animals are to dwell in. Matthew 5:48 say's *"Therefore be perfect, as your heavenly father is perfect".* If He did it for the animals then He expects you to provide for the animals that are in your care that same seventy-five degree environment give or take five degree's. Then sow your cost as a seed, and watch God bless you.

Many times God uses different situations to test us. *"Work hard and cheerfully at whatever you do, as though you were working for the Lord"* (Col. 3:23). Know this, that what good that you do Jesus Christ will reward you here on earth, He is faithful.

He's the only person you need to care about what He thinks, including what you do or how you do it, especially when no one is looking, because God is. He's your only judge and the only one you need to impress. *"For the Lord does not see as man sees, for man looks at the outward appearance, but the Lord looks at the heart"* (1 Sam. 6:7).

The point is whether you believe it or not, God does know what you're thinking, hello! Believe me, if you pass one of the many tests that God will present to you, then He will promote you to a higher level. All promotions come from God, but they always come with a test first. *"He delights in you and has placed you on the throne to rule for Him"* (2 Chron. 9:8). God puts kings on thrones. So the next time you're in a situation where you see a stray cat, dog, or any kind of animal abuse, stop and think, *Is this a test from God, and how can I do this so that it is pleasing to Him?*

In many cases, this will require more of what Christians call the "killing of the flesh." This means that your flesh will want to do one thing and be in fear, and the Holy Spirit will be convicting your spirit to do another. It's during these times of being in what we Christians call the fire in a trial that an individual's lack of spiritual maturity, along with his or her integrity, and/or respect for the animal kingdom, will be exposed. Christians call trials fire because our fleshly nature wants to do one thing, and when you don't let it, then our bodies feel like they are in a lot of physical pain.

And for the record, if you're a Christian who is filled with the Holy Spirit, it is wise to be Spirit led, not flesh led. Some people are not strong enough to say no to their flesh, and so they have unwittingly let chains, yokes, and bondages erect themselves in their lives and finances. It's important to be Spirit ruled only by the Holy Spirit. Sin leads only one way—to destruction. After people sin, they wonder why their lives are so bad and nothing works out right for them. There are many areas where people sin. I'm only dealing with your sin with the animals in your life. Some of you can start by taking a good look outside of your window into your backyard and look at that animal that you've tortured by leaving it out in weather that not even God would leave them in. Then ask yourself, *Now, who's really in chains, me or that animal?* Part of the reason that many things are going wrong in your life. Can be attributed to the unrighteous way you treat the animals in your care or just animal period.

Sinning opens doors to the spirit world where devils can enter your life. They steal your money and your stuff, nothing gets paid, and everything is constantly going wrong. Ding, ding, ding—wake up, these are your red flags that you're doing something wrong. Can't you see it? The devil can also attack you when you're doing something right, but that is another teaching altogether. As you spiritually mature, you will see the difference. The point is if your animals are not getting love or attention and all their needs met the way God did for them in the Garden of Eden, then they're not living the quality life that God intended for them to be living. So you're in sin, and sin is bondage, and that means that you have a whole lot of chains, yokes, and yes, bondages that need to be removed from your life before you can begin to prosper.

I pray that this book opens your eyes to your door of freedom, because with a renewed mind to the truth, you can shake off those chains and walk free in a blessed and prosperous life. The spirit realm is the dominant and more powerful realm than the natural realm we live in every day. Why do you think that it's called the supernatural realm? It's because it's much more powerful than the everyday natural realm that we exist in. Jesus lived in this natural world, but He knew how to access and operate in the supernatural realm at all times. That's what He wants for us.

First John 5:18 says, *"We know that those who have become part of God's family do not make a practice of sinning, for God's Son holds them securely, and the evil one cannot get his hands on them."* Jesus knew that if He sinned then the devil could, by the laws that operate in this earth, attack him, so Jesus never sinned. When you sin, you become powerless, and you give the devil the authority to steal, kill, and destroy in your life. It's just like pulling an electrical plug out of the wall and now you have no power or protection. Likewise, when you don't sin, it's just like putting the plug back into the wall and now you have power and protection—and lots of it. You are now plugged into the free supernatural power that is available to all of us.

That same supernatural power, along with words, is what God used to make this universe. That's why God tells us not to be a slave to our flesh. It will cause you to sin and cut you off from all of heaven's supernatural power. God even gave us an instruction manual on how to access it to use it to get our needs met; it's called the Bible. Jesus even came down from glory to personally teach it to us. That's how much He loves us. Or you can operate by death's laws by sinning and speaking death words. These wrong words do not come back void. They manifest in this world, creating a powerless life where you are always struggling and never getting ahead and existing at the bottom forever.

One example of a death word is the word luck, like when people are at the bottom in their life and it's not going as well as they would like it to be, they say something like their luck has run out or that they are out of luck.

First, the word luck, which does not exist, was introduced into our speech to be a counterfeit to the real word *blessings*. This is God's Word. Deuteronomy 11:26–28 says, *"Today I am giving you the choice between a blessing and a curse! You will be blessed if you obey the commands of the Lord your God that I am giving you today. You will receive a curse if you reject the commandments of the Lord your God and turn from his way by worshiping foreign gods."* So also was the word karma introduced—I mean made up. It's a counterfeit word to steal away another of God's truths. The word karma is given the credit, not God's word, when people say such things as, "Well that's karma for you." Or "What comes around go's around" and "Now you're getting back what you did. It's all because of that karma." No it isn't. It's God's laws of blessings or curses operating in your life.

Galatians 6:7 says, *"Do not be deceived, God is not mocked; for what so ever a man sows, that he shall reap."* Believe me when I say to you that no one can outrun or hide from the manifestation of God's laws in this realm. I mean it. Proverbs 11:31 says, *"If the righteous receive their just due here on earth how much more will the ungodly and the wicked receive."*

When God first created the Garden of Eden on this earth, there was no sin in the world, no zoos, circuses, or cages. There were no chains on the animals that dwelt in the garden with Adam. My how times have changed.

The unsaved of this world believe that to be better than the next guy, they have to be first. This is a lie and a deadly belief system that frankly does not work with the laws of the very earth that they live on. Yet they repeatedly buck against the laws of this universe and cry when they don't get what they want. That's what I call crazy. If they would only apply the same energy to following the rules that are written in the Bible, they would soon see that these laws would actually set them free, and in a short time, they would start to see good progress and positive change manifest in their lives. Matthew 20:26–27 says, *"Yet it shall not be so among you; but whoever desires to become great among you, let him be your servant. And whoever desires to be first among you, let him be your slave."*

You see, God gave us a living, breathing example of how we are to be. He is Jesus. We are to be a servant to all—a servant to your husband, your wife, your children, and to the animals in your care, even to your friends and neighbors. In fact, many historical theologians also believed the Bible where it said that all animals could speak words in the Garden of Eden to communicate with Adam and Eve. Again i.e. the serpent in the Garden of Eden talking with Eve. It was not until Jehovah God's judgment on man and the animals of the earth when the serpent lied to Eve that God's judgment removed the animal's ability to speak words. It is only when words are spoken by a human being that word's then have the power to create. This will not happen when animals speak words. Animals were not made in the image of Jehovah God, we humans were. We have the power to create with our words like our father in heaven. It was also at this same exact time when all the animals became wild. The animals had no fear of humans in the Garden of Eden. All the animals just walked up to Adam so he could name them while in the Garden of Eden. This Scripture gives us a glimpse of the way all the animals will be living with us and Jesus Christ in the renewed earth to come. Isaiah 11:6–8 says:

> The wolf will live with the lamb, the leopard will lie down with the goat, the calf and the lion and the yearling together; and a little child will lead them. The cow will feed with the bear, their young will lie down together, and the lion will eat straw like the ox. The infant will play near the hole of the cobra, and the young child will put his hand into the vipers nest.

All animals and human beings were also vegetarians in the Garden of Eden. This is the way the world was supposed to operate, not just in the Garden of Eden but forever. I was watching TV one night, and I saw carnivores running down their prey and then killing it. When Jesus returns, we will never have to see or hear about death. This fall also caused the earth's degeneration in every area including the set temperature of the earth's climate that was always between a perfect 70-80 degrees at all times forever.

CHAPTER 3

ICE AGE—THE BIG HOAX!

In the days of Noah, God found Noah to be the only righteous man on earth. There was a race of giants, the seed of the serpent (i.e., the devil), that was multiplying and spreading across the world, teaching man all kinds of unrighteousness. This is the only reason Jehovah God flooded the entire world, to destroy this demonic race of giants. Evolutionists and the secular world attached this word evolve to the human race and to the plants and animals. This is wrong and should never have happened. Man, plants, and the animals are exactly the way God created them almost seven thousand years ago. Animals have had to try and adapt to their environments, and in these environments they die sooner, but that's not evolving!

And as for an ice age, there never was a so-called ice age. An ice age never happened. This is a fictitious event. If there ever was such a thing as an ice age, it would have been recorded in the Bible, just like the flood and Noah's ark, but there is no record of such an event. The ice age is propaganda spewed out by evolutionists who believe in Darwin's lies. They also invented the word prehistoric. The beginning of when animal and man showed up on the earth was approximately a little less than seven thousand years ago. There is no such thing as cave men who came from apes. Yes, human beings have lived in caves, but that's all.

Humans also lived alongside all the dinosaurs. The dinosaurs showed up in Genesis when God created the animals from the dust of the earth. Dinosaurs are nothing more than large land animals. These Darwinians also don't believe that Jesus is the Messiah. They don't believe that He was God in the flesh when He walked on this earth two thousand years ago either. I believe that there is a gap. You know the time between Genesis 1:1 and Genesis 1:2. It is this gap in time when the devil and the 1/3 of God's angels were cast to the earth. I believe this to be where the secular world gets these 200 million, 400 million years and so forth numbers from. *I do not believe it was 10, 200-400 million years or any year past seven thousand years for the age of any dinosaur bone.* The devil and the fallen angels existed here on the earth during those millions of years however long we do not know. But then the Holy Spirit shows up in Genesis 1:2 to start to re-new the earth. These misinformed people would have you believe that the Bible is a lie. These people are lying to you and to themselves. Anyone who would say that man and animals lived before Genesis 1:2 does not believe the Bible in the literal sense.

The fact is that the Bible interprets the Bible all by itself. For example, God explains twenty-seven times that the beast is always a man. Second Peter 1:21 says, *"For prophecy never had its origin in the will of man, but men spoke from God as they were carried along by the Holy Spirit."* Rev. Billy Graham and Rev. Jack Van Impe, to just name a couple, both believe the Bible literally. Spiritually mature Christians believe that the Word of God is God breathed.

Genesis 1:2 says, *"Now the earth was formless and empty, darkness was over the surface of the deep, and the Spirit of God was hovering over the waters."* Genesis 1:2 took place a little less than only seven thousand years ago. Yes, the earth was formless and in darkness pre-Genesis 1:2. The devil and one-third of the fallen angels inhabited it, but there were definitely no man, animals, plants, or the earth and sky as we know them now. We don't know just how long the devil and his minions existed here. Christians believe that the universe and the human race with the animals are not all just happenstance. This universe and everything in it didn't just all fall together or just happen. Genesis 1:1 says, *"In the beginning God created the heavens and the earth."*

The truth is we don't know if the gap between Genesis 1:1 & Genesis 1:2 was 10 million or 400 million years. But we who believe the Bible know for a fact that the animals, which includes all the dinosaurs and mankind did not show up on this earth until the Garden of Eden and that's after Genesis 1:2. This is exactly how the devil works. He thinks that saying a lie over and over and over again will somehow or someday make it the truth. It won't; a lie will always be a lie, just like the truth will always be the truth. Second Corinthians 10:5 says, *"Casting down arguments and every high thing that exalts itself against the Word of God, bringing every thought into captivity to the obedience of Christ."*

The Garden of Eden was being created almost seven thousand years ago in Genesis 1:2. This is a demonic antichrist spirit working in the world today. This demonic spirit uses unsaved people to makeup all of these lies. The numbers of 10,150, 200, 400 million years is probably the amount of time that the devil and his demons existed alone in the cold dark formless void before Genesis 1:2.

I truly believe this is where these millions and billions of years are coming from in the secular world. It's the demons themselves working through unsaved people. The devil in these people has also made up the word prehistoric and the word luck. All these new words that demons create, which are added to our words, are all to steal God's credit. It goes on and on.

The Darwinians and evolutionists made up a perverted version of human beings by using a tooth that they found. But after they have done further research on this so-called Neanderthal, they now know that the tooth is only the tooth of a pig. This information came from an article called "The Scientific Evidence for the Origin of Man" written by David N. Menton, a PhD from St. Louis, Missouri, in 1988. You can go to Missouri Association for Creation—the Origin of Man for more information on this subject. Even to this day the atheists still display these wax perversions of the God-created human being in their museums and call them Neanderthals. Atheists try to say that Jehovah God created human beings from apes. The funny thing is that the missing link to uphold this crazy theory has never been found.

Now I'm confused; which is it? Do they want us to believe that we came from pond scum or apes? I was watching Dr. Carl Baugh, a Christian Creation expert who can be seen on the Trinity Broadcasting Network (TBN) and Daystar, had a Christian doctor of mathematics who had researched secular scientists' findings on the genes of the human race. And this Christian doctor of mathematics showed the secular scientists' own findings and announcements in their own scientific journals. Their research found that every human being's gene can be traced back to one woman within the last seven thousand years, and her name is Eve. Genesis 3:20 says, "*Then Adam named his wife Eve, because she would be the mother of all people everywhere.*"

Darwinians and evolutionists don't want you to believe that the human race was created by God. They want you to believe that we all came from apes or pond scum or anything, as long as it's not from God. They go so far as to put ape jaws and ape bones into their fake wax sculptures in museums, and then they say that the human race evolved from apes also. This is all pure fiction. All Christians must know the Word of God very well to see through their lies. Here are some more lies that evolutionists make up to explain how all the dinosaurs and animals that were not on the ark became extinct. First, some dinosaur eggs were carried onto the ark.

For further research, you can check out http://www.creationevidence. org by Dr. Carl Baugh. Evolutionists, Darwinians, and atheists have their theory of an ice age or a meteor from outer space that killed all the dinosaurs instead of the real truth, which is that the flood of Noah alone killed all the land animals that were not on the ark of Noah. It's a spirit of confusion straight from the devil; it has his MO all over it. It's through all of these lies that the devil tries to steal God's credit for the creation of the earth, the creation of the universe, and the flood of Noah that caused the extinction of all the animals from the face of the earth. This spirit tries to pass these lies of propaganda off to the human race in the media. These lies are all a counterfeit of God's truth the Bible.

There are demonic spirits that are operating in anyone who rejects the Bible and who also doesn't believe that the flood of Noah alone carved out the Grand Canyon, which it did. What spirit do you see operating inside of all these people? It's sure not the Holy Spirit. God does not steal. John

10:10 says, *"The thief [devil] does not come except to steal, and to kill, and to destroy."* The devil tries to steal the Word of God from people's hearts by using counterfeit words and sayings and mixes them with half-truths, which are out-and-out lies.

In these next Bible verses, this is God talking. He says in Genesis 6:17–22, 7:1–24, and 8:1–21:

"Look! I am about to cover the earth with a flood that will destroy every living thing. Everything on the earth will die! But I solemnly swear to keep you safe in a boat, with your wife and your sons and their wives. Bring a pair of every kind of animal—a male and a female—into the boat with you to keep them alive during the flood. Pairs of each kind of bird and of each kind of animal, large and small alike will come to you to be kept alive. And remember take enough food for your family and for all the animals." So Noah did everything exactly as God had commanded him. Finally, the day came when the Lord said to Noah, "Go into the boat with all your family, for among all the people of the earth, I consider you alone to be righteous. Take along seven pairs of each animal that I have approved for eating and for sacrifice, and take one pair of each of the others. Then select seven pairs of every kind of bird. There must be a male and a female in each pair to ensure that every kind of living creature will survive the flood. One week from today I will begin forty days and forty nights of rain. And I will wipe from the earth all the living things I have created." So Noah did exactly as the Lord had commanded him. He was six hundred years old when the flood came, and he went aboard the boat to escape—he and his wife and his sons and their wives. With them were all the various kinds of animals, those approved for eating and sacrifice and those that were not along with all the birds and other small animals. They came into the boat in pairs, male and female, just as God had commanded Noah. One week later, the flood came and covered the earth.

When Noah was six hundred years old, on the seventeenth day of the second month, the underground waters burst forth on the earth, and rain fell in mighty torrents from the sky. The rain continued to fall for forty days and for forty nights. But Noah had gone into the boat that very day with his wife and his sons—Shem, Ham, and Japheth—and their wives. With them in the boat were pairs of every kind of breathing animal—domesticated and wild, large and small—along with birds and flying insects of every kind. Two by two they came into the boat, male and female, just as God had commanded. Then the Lord shut them in. For forty days the flood prevailed, covering the ground and lifting the boat high above the earth. As the water rose higher and higher above the ground, the boat floated safely on the surface. Finally, the water covered even the highest mountains on the earth, standing more than twenty-two feet above the highest peaks. All the living things on earth died—birds, domestic animals, wild animals, all kinds of small animals, and all the people. Everything died that breathed and lived on dry land. Every living thing on the earth was wiped out—people, animals both large and small, and birds. They were all destroyed, and only Noah was left alive, along with those who were with him in the boat. And the water covered the earth for 150 days. But God remembered Noah and all the animals in the boat. He sent a wind to blow across the waters, and the floods began to disappear. The underground water sources ceased their gushing, and the torrential rains stopped. So the flood gradually began to recede. After 150 days, exactly five months from the time the flood began, the boat came to rest on the mountains of Ararat. Two and a half months later, as the waters continued to go down, other mountain peaks began to appear. After another forty days, Noah opened the window he had made in the boat and released a raven that flew back and forth until the earth was dry. Then he sent out a dove to see if it could find dry ground. But the dove found no place to land because the water was still too high, so it returned to the boat, and Noah held out his hand and drew the dove back inside. Seven days later, Noah released the dove again. This time, toward evening, the bird returned to him with a fresh olive leaf in its beak. Noah now knew that the water was almost gone. A week later, he released the dove again, and this time it did not come back. Finally, when Noah was 601 years old, ten and a half months after the flood began Noah lifted back the cover to look. The water was drying up. Two more months went by, and at last the earth was dry! Then God said to Noah, "Leave the boat, all of you. Release all the animals and the birds so they can breed and reproduce in great numbers." So Noah and his wife and his sons and their wives left the boat. And all the various kinds of animals and birds came out, pair by pair. Then Noah built an altar to the Lord and sacrificed on it the animals and the birds that had been approved for that purpose. And the Lord was pleased with the sacrifice and said to Himself, "I will never again curse the earth, destroying all living things, even though people's thoughts and actions are bent toward evil from childhood; nor will I again destroy every living thing as I have done." God wanted to start over again, so He baptized the whole earth with water. And He also made a brand new covenant with the people and the animals that came off the ark and with the earth.

Genesis 9:13–16 says:

"And as for me, behold, I establish my covenant with you and with your descendants after you, and with every living creature that is with you: the birds, the cattle, and every beast of the earth with you, of all that go out of the ark, every beast of the earth. Thus I establish my covenant with you: Never again shall all flesh be cut off by the; waters of the flood never again shall there be a flood to destroy the earth." And

God said: "This is the sign which I make between me and you, and every living creature that is with you, for perpetual generations: I set my rainbow in the cloud, and it shall be a sign of the covenant between me and the earth."

A catastrophic flood covered the whole earth, and it was caused by Jehovah God, not an ice age and not a meteor from outer space. God had to destroy the seed of Satan, a race of giants that were overpopulating the earth and leading man into all kinds of astrology and satanic worship, acts of murder, and perverted sexual behavior. But Jehovah God didn't want to lose all the animals or humans on this planet, so he instructed Noah and his family members, a total of eight people, to build the ark. God waited 120 years for Noah to build that huge ark. It was longer than a football field and three stories high. God loves the animals so much that He did not want all of them to become extinct, so the angels of the Lord were assigned by God to go out and bring in the exact number and type of animals that God would use to repopulate the earth with. If God went out of His way to preserve the animals of this earth, than who are we to be higher than God? Genesis 1:22 says, *God created the animals and blessed them."*

The Word says in 2 Corinthians 3:18, *"And we, who with unveiled faces all reflect the Lord's glory, are being transformed into ever increasing glory, which comes from the Lord, who is the Spirit."* You know those wrist bands that say, *"What would Jesus do?"* Well, Jesus would never treat the animals of this world the way that we have. And while I'm thinking about it. If the ground is too hot or cold for your hand when you touch it. Then it's defiantly too hot or cold for your animal's feet. You see at between 70-80 degrees the ground in the Garden of Eden would always feel perfect.

CHAPTER 4

SEVENTY-FIVE DEGREES

Some might be asking, "Where did you get the seventy-five degrees for the temperature in the Garden of Eden? It's right there in the Bible.

Genesis 2:25 says, *"The man (Adam) and his wife was both naked, and they felt no shame."* There it is—they were naked and thought there was nothing wrong with not being covered up.

This Scripture clearly reveals that God prepared a climate set at a temperature that was comfortable enough for naked human bodies to thrive in and to be sustained in for eternity. Remember now, it was not until after they sinned by eating the fruit from the Tree of Knowledge of Good and Evil that all of creation was cursed. Even that perfect climate started to degenerate from that moment on.

Adam and Eve ate from the Tree of Knowledge of Good and Evil, and then they felt that they needed clothes. Genesis 3:7 says, *"Then the eyes of both of them, Adam and Eve were opened, and they realized they were naked; so they sowed fig leaves together and made coverings for themselves."* That Scripture also reveals that if Adam and Eve had never eaten from the Tree of Knowledge of Good and Evil, then they would have lived naked forever *"because they felt no shame"*.

I don't know about you but I could not exist naked in any other temperature other than between seventy and eighty degrees comfortably.

Could you? Remember you're naked now, and you would never think of covering up because you feel no shame.

Here is another eye opener. Genesis 3:11 says, *"And He [God] said, 'Who told you that you were naked? Have you eaten from the tree that I commanded you not to eat from?'"*

That Scripture is dealing with two questions in one Scripture from God to Adam and Eve. The first question God asks is, "Who were you talking to?" I'm not dealing with that question right now. What I am addressing is the other question that God is asking in that same Scripture to Adam and Eve. God is asking Adam and Eve, "What has happened to you both that you now all of a sudden believe that it is wrong to be naked?" You see, even Jehovah God is asking them, "Why do you both think it strange now to be naked, because you didn't before?" It's clear that God intended for all of mankind to exist for eternity naked, because they were not ashamed before, not until after their eyes were opened. If Adam and Eve's eyes were never opened, they and all their family members would have continued on into eternity naked, not knowing anything different.

God created this world for us all to be comfortable, without want, and with all of our needs met, and that includes the animals. They were created to be tame, not wild, to eat grass and leaves, not each other. He also intended for the climate to always be perfect and comfortable for them. God never intended for humans or animals to be sick or thirsty. His desire was for all of man and animals to have all their needs met all the time. They were to never experience hunger. That also means that there would never have been scavengers. There was an abundance of everything, and nothing would have ever run out. God made provision for them in the Garden that was to last for eternity. So for us as believers, to subject any animal that we own to life-threatening elements is sinful. If God didn't do it, then don't you do it.

I hear all the time now the media is crying about how the climate is changing, and they scare everyone with their new phrase, "global warming." Their latest slogan is, "Let's all go green."

Second Peter 3:8–13 says:

"With the Lord a day is like a thousand years, and a thousand years is like a day." The Lord isn't really being slow about His promise to return, as some people think. No, he is being patient for your sake. He does not want anyone to perish, so he is giving more time for everyone to repent. But the day of the Lord will come unexpectedly as a thief. Then the heavens will pass away with a terrible noise, and everything in them will disappear in fire, and the earth and everything on it will be exposed to judgment. Since everything around us is going to melt away, what holy, Godly lives you should be living! You should look forward to that day and hurry it along—the day when God will set the heavens on fire and the elements will melt away in the flames. But we [Christians] are looking forward to the new heavens and the new earth he has promised, a world where everyone is right with God. That also means that the earth's climate and weather will be right with Jesus our Lord God. He will again re- set the thermostat of this earth back to stay between 70-80ty degrees.*

Malachi 4:1–2 says:

The Lord Almighty says, "The day of judgment is coming, burning like a furnace. The arrogant and the wicked will be burned up like straw on that day. They will be consumed like tree- roots and all. But for you [Christians] who fear my name, the sun of righteousness will rise with healing in his wings. And you will go free, leaping with joy like calves let out to pasture. On the day when I act you will tread upon the wicked as if they were dust under your feet," says the Lord Almighty.

Matthew 5:5 says, *"Blessed are the meek [Christians] for they shall inherit the earth."* Yes, I do agree—let's not make this earth or the air anymore toxic to live in while we are here waiting for Jesus' return. What I don't agree with is the mindset that we could ever save this world by our own strength. Finding cleaner ways to produce and run things and to recycle is a wonderful start in the right direction. Whenever God gives you something, He expects you to take care of it, and that includes this earth. But more importantly, it's your soul that you really need to be worrying about, not this earth. Jesus promises in His Word that He will make all things new again.

And there's something else that I would like to clarify. In the book of Revelation, whenever you read the word *forever*, it is a literal forever. The words forever and ever in the book of Revelation mean that the judgment pronounced on the wicked is final. It stands forever, and it cannot be overturned or changed. After the wicked have been thrown into the lake of fire, they will simply be separated from God forever. We all should be thankful that because of God's great mercy all these years, we are not consumed daily. God has given mankind seven thousand years to repent. If anyone goes into the lake of fire, it will not be God's fault. It will be the fault of that stiff-necked person who had a stone cold heart. He or she never wanted to answer that still, small voice of Jesus knocking at the door of his or her heart. God is and always will be blameless.

God has given us all the rules to live by. They are designed to protect and prosper us. It's called the Bible. Proverbs 12:10 says, *"A righteous man cares for the needs of his animals."* Proverbs 16:7 says, *"When a man's ways are pleasing to the Lord he makes even our enemies live at peace with us."* Our enemy is the devil in this realm. Disobedience to God's Word opens doors in the supernatural realm. These doors are what the devil uses to come into a person's life and destroy anything that is good in a person's life. If we were to stand back and take a look at the animals of this earth right in this day and age, we would see them with collars on, and they would be in cages. It was not like that in the Garden of Eden. I can see what's wrong with that picture. Can you? But more importantly, what are you going to do about it?

Look around your life and get all known sin out of it, and if you still don't know what is considered sin, buy a New International Version Bible on DVD and renew your mind to the truth. You will begin to see where sin has snuck in and has set up house in your life. You see, these spiritual bondages show up in a person's life in the form of a lack of finances, marital and relationship problems, and so forth. You get the picture. It literally clogs up and delays God's blessings that were originally on their way to you. If you will read the Word of God—I prefer the New International Version—follow what it teaches, and make all the necessary changes in and around your life, then you will start to see all your blessing from God loosed from demonic attacks and theft, for the Word says in Hosea 4:6, *"My people die for the lack of knowledge."*

CHAPTER 5

STOP PERVERTING WHAT GOD HAS CREATED!

B ear with me here because I'm going back to animals with this. Have you ever wondered where all that wonderful taste and all the vitamins and minerals went too, that use to be in our fruits and vegetables before the 1950s? I'm going to answer that question for you right now. Because healthy, thin people never made anybody any money, but unhealthy, overweight people make big business billions of dollars. Big business removes more than two-thirds of that sumptuous taste from all the fruits and vegetables that we eat and injects unhealthy hormones into the flesh of the animals that we eat. All this to turn people to eat processed food, which has no nutritional value and is made to make us unhealthy and overweight. Leviticus 20:19 says, *"You must obey all my laws. Do not breed your cattle with other kinds of animals. Do not plant your field with two kinds of seed."*

The Bible clearly states that we are to not mix seeds. That means no human cloning, no animal cloning, and no plant cloning. This also means no mixing of their seeds. This makes hybrids. All this is an abomination to God. We are not to breed animals with human beings either. All of this is sin, and God will not bless sin. So if you're having problems in your research and experiments, this is your problem: you're sinning! There is always a high price to pay here in the land of the living for sin. Sin will not be denied. It always catches up with you here on earth, just like sin required payment when Adam and Eve sinned. But thank the Lord Jesus Christ for stepping down out of glory and paying that expensive price for all of us. So stop right now, and repent and have nothing to do with these ungodly projects. The Bible says, *"If you love me you will keep my Word. Choose this day whom you shall serve"* (Josh. 24:15). We must make a choice. Are we going to go along with the ways of the world, or are we going to obey the Word of God?

Another fact—have you noticed that this world stinks? I mean, it really smells bad. That's not by accident. If you're like me, you buy those scented plug-ins and candles. In the Garden of Eden, it smelled wonderful. Adam and Eve did not need to do anything to make the air that they breathed smell sweet because the flowers took care of that. Ladies—now I'm talking to the much older woman, someone who lived in the forties—do you remember when your boyfriend would buy you a bouquet of flowers and you took a big whiff of those roses and they smelled so wonderful?

Today that smell has been purposely bred right out of them by big business so you and billions of other people will buy their products. Really, go smell a rose from a flower shop. There is hardly any smell to them. I am fifty-one, and I can remember in the early sixties when I smelled flowers, they gave off a powerful aroma. Now mass-produced flowers have very little aroma to them anymore. Yes, I've heard that before, during, and after the Rose Parade that the air smells sweet from the flowers. But that's nothing compared to the smell of a rose that has not been genetically altered in a lab. I would not be surprised at all if big business did not supply the people putting those floats together with rose-smelling spray to spay all over the floats when they are finished. One day, when I was buying some more of those things that you plug in to your light socket to make your house smell nice for only about three weeks, I thought to myself, *"Nobody needed these things in the fifties. What's happened"? "The flowers of the world are not doing their job anymore".*

And then the Holy Spirit answered me and said, *"The flowers were making the earth smell sweet, and it didn't cost anyone anything. Now to get that same sweet smell, big business forces billions of people to pay for something that I gave to them for free."*

CHAPTER 6

ALL ANIMALS SEE IN BRIGHT, VIVID COLOR

I've heard so-called animal experts say that all animals only see in black and white. I could tell by the words coming out of these animal experts' mouths that they were not saved, so I just went to the real expert, the Holy Spirit, and I asked him. This is what He told me: *"Man did not make the animals or this earth; I, Jehovah God, did. I created a vividly colored world. Just look at the many colors in all the tropical fish in the oceans. Look at the brightly colored birds, along with all the colorful animals of this earth. And look at the rich colors in the flowers all over the world. It wasn't until thousands of years later when, man made the first black-and-white picture. Man then made the first black-and-white movies. And then man also made the first black-and-white TV shows. All the animals on this earth were created by me, Jehovah God, not man, to see the world just like humans were created to see it—in bright, vivid color."*

God did not create a black-and-white world. He made a world full of color, so why would God ever create anything to see in black and white when the world is in color? A chameleon changes it skin color to protect its self from predators to look like the color of its surroundings. If that chameleon cannot see in color then how come that same chameleon always picks the exact color of its surroundings to look like," It's because it can see in bright vivid color's that's why".

We do not serve a broke, stingy, or cruel God who just decided on the fifth day of creating the earth that He would start cutting corners when making the animals and make them so that they could not see in color. When you read the Bible, you get to know God's personality. You will also find out that He's an over-the-top kind of God. He's a more-than-enough kind of God. Even the angels can see this beautiful masterpiece in all its grandeur in color.

God wants all of us and the animals to enjoy looking at the beautiful colors of this world. In fact, if you haven't already noticed, it's the animals and the birds that are more colorful than the human race. Why would God make the animals so colorful and then not let them see and enjoy looking at each other? That makes no sense at all. Animals use their coloring to arouse and attract each other to mate with or to scare predator's away.

The Word says, *"We are to look around and to keep all sin out of our lives."* Matthew 18:8–9 says:

> *If your hand or foot causes you to sin, cut it off and cast it from you. It is better for you to enter into life maimed, rather than having two hands or two feet, to be cast into the everlasting fire. And if your eye causes you to sin, pluck it out and cast it from you. It is better for you to enter into your life with one eye, rather than having two eyes and to be cast into hell fire.*

If you believe that the life of any animal is worthless, I have a God who says otherwise. All through the Bible it talks about what God thinks of the animals The Garden of Eden is just one example of how God took care of the animals. They had a comfortable environment that was safe for them to live in, and everything was plentiful. They lacked nothing.

We are all subject to God's Word and commandments. They are life to us. God does the best that He can for the wild animals in a fallen world. Deuteronomy 10:14 says, *"The earth and all that is in it belongs to the Lord."* Luke 12:24 says, *"Consider the ravens they do not sow or reap, and they have no storerooms or barns, yet God feeds them."* We are to be imitators of God, so what are you doing to God's creatures? Think to yourself, *"Is what I'm doing good and loving, or is it cruel and wicked"?* Your actions and your words are seeds.

For example, when you leave for work, is someone home to care for your animals, such as a dog, or have you provided a doggie door that only opens for them? Or have you abandoned them to a life of pain and torture to live outside in the freezing cold or unbearable heat? You will reap an abundant harvest of blessings in the here and now or you will receive abundant harvests of curses; it's your choice. When I hear or see people sin, I think to myself, *"Well, it's their own, 30, 60, and 100 fold grave that they're digging".* They'll be laying in it figuratively speaking, but literally, they will be in this world with chains and bondages erected in their lives. And they will have to contend with all the harvests from that sin.

You can tell some people all about the Word of God, but you can't make anyone adhere to it. That's the Holy Spirit's job. As a minister of the gospel, I'm just the messenger. It's the Holy Spirit that convicts people's hearts of the errors in their lives. It's the Holy Spirit that judges our hearts, and nothing can be hidden. So if you're saying in your heart to yourself, *"Oh, no one will ever find out or no one will ever know",* you're lying to yourself.

CHAPTER 7

THE NATURAL REALM VERSUS THE SPIRITUAL REALM

The fact is that everything you think, say, or do is put immediately into your book of record. And your book, along with everyone else's book of record, will be opened on the last day of this age, known as the Day of Judgment. You could say that we each have our own private stenographer. It's the Holy Spirit recording everything we say, do, or think—all of it, the good, the bad, and the ugly. But if we've accepted Jesus as our King and Savoir, His Word promises that after being born again, experiencing the new spiritual birth, and repenting for all of our sins, our sins are now and forever washed and covered with His blood. It says that on the Day of Judgment when our books of record are opened, God will not see any of our sins on those pages because they will appear as white as snow and will be covered by the blood of Jesus Christ.

That's why Christians are called "*saved*" a supernatural transformation happens. It's the power of the Holy Spirit that changes that once dead or cursed spirit of whoever accepts Jesus as their Lord and savior back to life in that moment. That's also why Christians are called born again. Our spirits are now alive again and can now enter heaven. The fact is that nothing dead can ever enter heaven. That is why all people must be born again to ever get into heaven. Your spirit will live forever with Jesus for eternity or be separated from Him forever in Hell. Yes, your body will get old and die if you're not saved, meaning your spirit has not been reborn or regenerated yet. If you are born again, the Word says that your body will be transformed in the twinkling of an eye and raptured.

Our body is just a coat that we wear to live and operate in this world. Jesus said to Nicodemus that every person must be born again to enter the Kingdom of God. When Jesus returns again, He promises that the people who accepted Him as their King and Savior will receive in a twinkling of an eye new, imperishable bodies to go with their new, born-again spirits into heaven. Death cannot enter heaven, nor can sin or anything that is cursed. First Corinthians 15:45–57 says:

> *And so it is written, the first Adam the spiritual is not first, but the natural, and afterward the spiritual. The first man was of the earth, made of the dust; the second Man is the Lord from heaven. As was the man of dust, so also are those who are made dust; and as is the heavenly Man, so also are those who are heavenly. And as we have borne the image of the man of dust [Adam], we shall also bear the image of the heavenly Man [Jesus]. Now this I say brethren that flesh and blood cannot inherit the kingdom of God; nor does corruption inherit incorruption. Behold, I tell you a mystery: We shall not all sleep, but we [the saved] shall all be changed—in a moment, in the twinkling of an eye, at the last trumpet. For the trumpet will sound, and the dead [all who chose Jehovah God and Jesus before they died] will be raised incorruptible, and we shall be changed. For this corruptible must put on incorruption, and this mortal must put on immortality. So when this corruptible has put on incorruption, and this mortal has put on immortality, then shall be brought to pass the saying that is written: "Death is swallowed up in victory." "O Death, where is your sting? O Hades, where is your victory?" The sting of death is sin, and the strength of sin is the law. But thanks be to God, who gives us [the saved] the victory through our Lord Jesus Christ.*

When Adam and Eve sinned, that sin caused a curse on the seed of the entire human race. In other words, Adam's seed was now infected. Adam was the first Adam and became a natural man. Jesus is the second Adam and is a spiritual and supernatural man forever. Another huge difference between Adam and Jesus is that Jesus didn't sin or fall to any temptations, unlike Adam, who failed. Romans 5:19 says, *"For as by one Man's disobedience many were made sinners, so also by one Man's obedience [Jesus] many will be made righteous."*

That's why we are all in need of a Savior. We humans weren't given the power or the authority to forgive any sin, let alone our own sins. That power and authority was given by God to His only Son, Jesus Christ of Nazareth. Acts 10:42–43 says, *"And he ordered us to preach everywhere and to testify that Jesus is ordained of God to be the judge of all—the living and the dead. He is the one all the prophets testified about, saying that everyone who believes in him will have their sins forgiven through his name."*

CHAPTER 8

WHAT IS BIGFOOT AND
WHERE DID IT COME FROM?

They are known by many names: ***Bigfoot, Sasquatch, Skunk ape, The Legend of Boggy Creek, Yeti. The Abominable Snowman, The Loch ness Monster and yes, Space Alien's.*** The fact is that they are all one and the same. They are very, very real, and they are very, very dangerous. These are the names they are called now, but they went by other names over 5,000 years ago when they walked in the flesh on this earth. They were called giants, the Nephilim, or demons in the flesh. A race of giants inhabited the Promised Land and most parts of the world.

Josephus was a historian back in the 1900s wrote: "*For which reason they removed their camp to Hebron; and when they had taken it they slew all the inhabitants. They told of a race of giants that had bodies so large and their countenance was so entirely different from that of human men. These giants had six toes and six fingers on each of their hands and feet. It was also said that when these giants spoke it was terrible to the hearing. The bones of these giants were on display 1900 years ago. The records revealed that they were unlike any credible relations to any human man.* Josephus, Book V, Chapter II. It was for this reason that Jehovah God flooded the earth in the days of Noah. It was to annihilate these seeds of Satan who were teaching mankind all sorts of demon worship, blood sacrifices, and wickedness.

Sin was already in the world before Adam and Eve were ever created and put into the Garden of Eden. Satan had been cast down like lighting with a third of the angels to the earth. They were all condemned to the lowest status of all: fallen angels. Lucifer was now Satan, God's angels were now demons, and both as soon as they left heaven like lighting became hideous in appearance and their purpose changed to perversions of ungodliness.

When Adam and Eve were tempted by the devil in the Garden of Eden and fell into sin, it was at this time that Jehovah God pronounced judgment on the human race. Genesis 3:15 says, *"I will put enmity between you [the devil] and the woman, between your seed [the devil's seed] and her [the woman's seed], it shall bruise your head [the devil's head] and you shall bruise her [the woman's] heel."* Genesis 6:2 *"that the sons of God saw the daughters of men, that they were beautiful; and they took wives for themselves of all whom they chose."*

There are three groups of angels; the first group, were the third of the angels that fell like lighting to the earth with Satan (Ezek. 28:14–-17, Luke 10:18). The second group of angels the 200 of Jehovah God's angels came down to teach man the ways of righteousness again. This is not the devils 1/3 of the fallen angels. This is God's 200 angels who took on the form of man. This is when the devils fallen angels who are demonic spirits tempted Jehovah God's angels who are now in the form of man all fell into sin, and took in marriage and slept with the daughters of men. Because God's 200 angels went into the daughters of men. This union produced a perverted race of beings called *Giants.* Jehovah God punished his 200 angels who had fallen into sin and who had slept with the daughters of men producing these *Giants* and He cast them into Tatarus. This is a chamber near the center of the earth where the worst demons are bound until they are released back into the earth during the seven year tribulation to torment men.

To wipe from the face of the earth this unholy race of giants (the seed of Satan), Jehovah God flooded the entire earth. As the giants (the seed of Satan) drowned in the flood of Noah, their demonic spirits were released into the spirit realm of this earth, where they remain to this day. These are the same demonic spirits that people chase in houses and out in the mountains. When humans or animals die, their spirits are not on this earth.

They are not left behind or lost. ***They do not have the power to reappear or communicate with us in any way, shape, or form on this earth.***

Gen. 6:4 " *"there were giants on the earth in those days, and also afterwards. When the sons of Jehovah God **(His two hundred angels)** came into the daughters of men and bore children to them. Those were the mighty men who were of old, men of renown."* Even to this day in **2011** the legend of them is still talked about everyone sees them in our children's movies and cartoons. Their fame is kept alive in commercials, movies and on T.V. They are what is presently known as those **legendary Greek gods in books, they are not legends they were real!** They really existed just not the way you thought they existed. The serious problem is that man should never ever worship them. But they did and still do. Worshiping these **so called**, *Greek gods* **is <u>sin against Jehovah God</u>**. So you can imagine how this really got out of hand and how famous they had become even back then. They were worshipped and idolized by man back then and still even to this day, still by some. You see Jehovah God is a jealous God. No wonder Jehovah God only mentioned their fame in one fleeting blip in a sentence.

Let's re-cap remember these are God's angels now not the devils first group that fell with him. Two hundred of God's angels came down to the earth. And they took on the image of man and fell into sin. They could not resist the daughters of men, they slept with the daughters of men and married them as they pleased. Now God's angels falling into sin and sleeping with the daughters of men produced a perverted race of beings a race of giants. This is where all the Greek myths of gods originated from that we hear about today. You see, in ancient times people thought that anything that came down from heaven was some type of god.

Let's compare the parallels of **Biblical facts, Greek mythology, Giants, Big foot, U.F.O's** an**d Demonic Spirits** that have been present on this earth since the great flood of Noah.

<u>Biblical Facts:</u> Two hundred of Jehovah God's angels touched down to the earth high on top of Mt. Hermon, one of the highest mountains. Jehovah God's angels dwelt on Mt. Hermon, took on the form of man, and soon fell into sin. These now-fallen angels went by all the names that are recorded in Greek mythology, such as Zeus, Hercules, and so forth. They were worshiped as gods by the people of the earth. They had supernatural powers, and they were very great in stature. They could not resist the daughters of men and took them as they pleased in marriage.

God cast these angels into Tatarus where they are bound to this day to be loosed during the seven year tribulation.

Greek Mythology: Their gods were worshiped by the people of the earth, and their gods also dwelt on top of the highest of mountains. In Greek myths, their gods had supernatural powers. Their gods were very large in stature, and they had great strength. And their gods could not resist the beauty of the daughters of man and took for themselves wives as they pleased.

Yes, there were giants on the earth before and after the flood of Noah. They show up again in the book of numbers. The point in this chapter is where did the Bigfoots, Sasquatches, along with the other names that I mentioned with them, come from? Not what order a book in the Bible was written. That's a whole other study. First there were the devils fallen angels. Second there was God's two hundred angels taking on the form of man and fell into sin, then sleeping with the daughters of men. For more in depth study of giants and angels read the book of Enoch, it's not in the Bible but Jesus loved Enoch so much and believed Enoch to be a righteous man. The off-spring of God's two hundred angels, whenever they died then their bodies released into the earth evil spirits which are present today. These unholy unions by Gods angels were the devils plan to stop the birth of Jesus (the seed of Jehovah God) from ever coming into this world.

The third group of angels is Jehovah God's angels who are still to this day in His heavenly service.

Giants: Let's explore the biblical presence of giants on the earth before and after the flood. These giants were as tall as twelve, fourteen, and eighteen feet tall. There are footprints that have been found from them that were thirty-six inches long. There was a giant named King Og and his bed was measured at eighteen feet long and made of iron. He is mentioned twenty-seven times in the Bible and ruled over sixty cities (Deut. 3:11).

Giants occupied many areas all over the Promised Land (Deut. 2:10–37, Deut. 3, Josh. 12:4–5).

Names of Giants
1. The Anakims possessed Hebron and Daber.
2. The Emims possessed beyond the Jordan River.
3. The Rephims possessed the Valley of Rephamin.
4. Avims possessed the Mediterranean coast.
5. The Zamzummins possessed the area of Jordan.

As a young boy, David killed the last of the giants in the flesh. That giant's name was Goliath (1 Sam. 17:1–58). Jesus took their power away in the spirit realm right after He died on the cross when He descended for three days into Hades (Matt. 12:40, Rev. 1:18).

Bigfoot: Those things that people are chasing on the television shows of today are the ***demonic spirits of dead giants***. That's why these ***Bigfoot's, Sasquatches, Skunk apes, The Legend of Boggy Creek, Yeti's, and the Abominable Snowman*** all have these very, very large footprints and handprints. And their chests are very, very large and they are all very, very tall. ***The Loch Ness Monster*** also is very, very large and is a demonic spirit, a ***shape shifter*** also.

U.F.O's: Some of these anomalies' are caused by demonic activity, after all the ***devil and his fallen angels*** and the ***demonic spirits from the dead offspring of God's two hundred fallen angels***, inhabit this earths' air space.

And some can be attributed to angelic activity; Jehovah God's angels are very, very busy with the work of the Lord.

Demons can manifest an image and produce demonic activity on the ***earth***, in the ***water*** and in the ***air*** and in ***outer space***. Test all spirits against the Word of Jehovah God.

Evil spirits from dead giants & Satan's demonic spirits: They are by no means as powerful as Jehovah God, Jesus Christ of Nazareth, or God's angels, but they can do some astonishing things and they have supernatural strength. The evil spirits that were released into the earth whenever a giant died are ***shape shifters*** they also have supernatural powers. They can appear as anything such as a deceased family member or a beloved pet. They can mimic their voices, their appearance, and any smell.

Inside a house or a building, people refer to them as *ghosts, entities, evil spirits, a lost soul, demonic spirits, and even a person or a deceased pet trying to communicate to them or to warn them.*

Outside when people see, smell, hear, or even have an encounter with them, they are referred to as *Sasquatch, Bigfoot, Skunk ape, The Legend of Boggy Creek, The Abominable Snowman*, and yes *Yeti, The Loch Ness Monster*, and *U.F.O's.*

People, they are *all one and the same.* They are the *demonic spirits of the dead giants of old.* They can physically hit you. They can push you down the stairs, leave scratches on your body, and move things. They can leave footprints and handprints and they will even let you photograph them.

They can create smells and sounds, they are *shape shifters*. They can kill your animals and pets, they can take passion of you or an animal and make you kill yourself. These demonic spirits can trick you into losing your very soul. Their only purpose is to do anything and everything it takes to get you to switch your focus off of Jesus Christ of Nazareth and for you to chase after them so that you lose your chance for salvation. They want you to be so obsessed with them to chase after them to worship them. People erect monuments to them and sell paraphernalia of them and make graven images of them and sell those images of them in gift shops. These demonic spirits have received worldwide notoriety, fame, and worship from the people of this earth.

All of this is breaking the first of the Ten Commandments which says Exodus 20: 1-2

"I am the Lord your God, who brought you out of the land of Egypt, out of the house of bondage. You shall have no other gods before me. "You shall not make for yourself a carved image, or any likeness of anything that is in heaven above, or that is in the earth beneath, or that is in the water under the earth; you shall not bow down to them nor serve them. For I, the Lord your God, am a jealous God, visiting the iniquity of the fathers on the children to the third and fourth generations of those who hate Me, but showing mercy to thousands, to those who love Me and keep My Commandments.

If you are preoccupied with *Satan's demonic spirits & the evil spirits, A.K.A shape shifters, from dead giants.* They are all betting that you will never accept Jesus as your King and savior and lose any chance for salvation. The devil and the fallen angels and demons will never be given the opportunity to receive salvation. But thanks to Jesus of Nazareth now every human has the opportunity to except this priceless free gift.So these *demonic spirits & evil spirits A.K.A shape shifters,* attack the very love of Jehovah God's heart that's you and I, the human race. They use miss focus and diversion's to keep as many human beings from receiving salvation from Jesus Christ. Salvation is the one thing that the devil and these evil spirits will never be given the opportunity to have. But it is offered to every human being as a free gift from Jesus Christ.

In the Bible, losing your soul is considered death. *It is everlasting separation from Jesus Christ of Nazareth.*

The reason why no one has ever found any natural evidence of them, nor will they ever find, a body or a body part not even a skeleton of one of these *evil spirits-/shape shifters.* It is because they are not *natural* they are *a perverted spiritual creature.* They are not *natural with flesh and blood* like human beings or animals. They are *spiritual*, straight from Satan, who tried to use them to stop the seed of Jehovah God (Jesus of Nazareth) from being born and save the human race.

CHAPTER 9

HIDDEN SNARES AND TRAPS IN MAN'S UNGODLY TRADITIONS

There are still some people who have this wrong way of thinking. I call it the inbred Jed way of thinking. They will tell you, *"Well that's the way my family's always treated animals, and so that's how I've been taught to do it also."* Colossians 2:20–23 says:

> *Since you [Christians] died with Christ, and He has set you free from the evil powers of this world. So why do you keep on following rules of the world, such as, "Don't handle, don't eat, don't touch." Such rules are mere human teaching about things that are gone as soon as we use them. These rules may seem wise because they require strong devotion, humility, and severe bodily discipline. But they have no effect when it comes to conquering a person's evil thoughts and desires.*

Matthew 15:9 says, *"Their worship is a farce, for they replace God's commands with their own man-made teachings."* Matthew 15:11 says, *"You are not defiled by what you eat; you are defiled by what you say and do."* In this chapter, I will go across the board and shed light on areas that have held many cultures in spiritual bondage. In some of these cultures, it's their tradition to drink the blood of animals. This is so sinful. Deuteronomy 12:23–25 says:

> *But be sure that you do not eat the blood, for the blood is the life; you may not eat the life with the meat. You shall not eat it; you shall pour it on the earth like water. You shall not eat it, that it may go well with you and your children after you, when you do what are right in the sight of the Lord.*

The blood contains all of the nutrition that your body needs to live. That is why in the Bible it is referred to as the blood of life. Do not be misled—the blood of animals or humans has no power in it other than when it is inside of a body to give it nutrition. Only the blood of Jesus Christ of Nazareth has supernatural powers, which come from Jehovah God, His father. Genesis 9:1–5 says, *"Just as I gave you the green plants, I now give you everything. But you must not eat meat that has its lifeblood still in it."* Now, there is no problem eating an animal to feed your family. The point here is that God is love, and He will not now or ever bless the torture or cruelty to any animal. If you kill any animal, do it in a humane, painless manner and only for food. Be careful what you do, lest your sins catch up with you. Trophy hunting for the sake of a trophy alone is sin. You trophy hunters aren't fooling anybody. God judges a man's heart. You're receiving your just due now in the land of the living. Galatians 6:7–9 says, *"Be not deceived God is not mocked whatsoever a man sows he shall reap in due season."* There are no seasons in heaven, only here on this earth. Proverbs 15:3 says, *"The eyes of the Lord are everywhere keeping watch on the wicked and the good."*

There's a horrible act that is done to innocent animals called vivisection. It's where so-called medical experiments are performed on live animals in the name of science. If sin had never been introduced into this world, we would never do such sinful things to God's animals. Please go to www. Peta.org. I want you to see the hidden video of what has been done to live animals to get that fur that you have. I stopped buying fur after I saw that video on the *PETA* website. I immediately went into my closet, took my knee-length white fox fur coat, shoved it into my fireplace, and burned it up. These animals could have been your pet dogs or cats.

I'll tell you, it's demonic spirits that people have operating through them that have caused this. But it's not those evil spirits that will pay the high price for their sin. It's the people who pay for it in the here and now. Not until the Day of Judgment will those demons get thrown into the lake off fire.

Governments sit passively by and do nothing. If these politicians weren't so bound with their own chains, yokes, and bondages that are choking their own economies, they might be able to do something to help them. There are also companies that are in huge sin and bondage. They have only cursed themselves. Until they stop, they will never prosper. How do I know? Because my Lord's Word tells me so.

There are other sins against animals. They include people who, for whatever reason, have sex with animals. This is called bestiality. Deuteronomy 27:21 says, *"Cursed is anyone who has sexual intercourse with an animal."* There are also demonic cults that go around mutilating farm animals and dogs and cats. It's all for their demon worship. The difference between their so-called god and the true and living God is that our God, Jesus, died for us and the devil expects you to die for him. Psalm 36: 6 says, *"Oh Lord, you preserve both man and beast."* Psalm 24:1 says, *"The earth is the Lords, and everything in it, for He found it upon the seas and established it upon the waters."* Psalm 8:6–9 says, *"You made Jesus, the ruler over the works of your hands, you put everything under Jesus, feet: all flocks and herds and the beasts of the field, the birds of the air, the fish of the seas. O Lord, our Lord, how majestic is your name in all the earth."*

I love to watch bull riding and while I was watching the show one night, I heard the announcer say that for this show they were up north and the temperature was in the thirties. I saw all the cowboys wearing heavy jackets and blowing into their hands to keep warm and jumping up and down. Now if these cowboys were that cold and were inside, I could just imagine how cold and in pain those bulls were. They are alive. They're not made of ceramic; they feel pain just like you and I do. Just as soon as I got done wondering where the bulls were, the camera showed the bulls standing outside in the freezing cold. The snow was falling onto the bulls, and you could see their hot breath blowing out of their noses into the cold air. I was having a hissy fit and screaming at the TV, "This is what I'm talking about, people! Wake up!"

This kind of treatment of animals makes me so mad! The owners of those bulls would make a whole lot more money if they didn't torture their animals. If they would only keep them in seventy-five degree trailers and barns. It doesn't matter if it's hot or cold outside. I know that the owners of those bulls are making some money off of them, but God's Word says that if you do things the way God shows you how, you will be blessed. Malachi 3:10 says, "*Then He will open the heavens and pour you out a blessing that you won't have room to contain.*" Like I said before, God will not bless torture, and that's torture. If God provided a seventy-five-degree environment for His bulls in the Garden of Eden, then you better do the same.

I also saw a show on television where a fish was cooked alive in a frying pan in a Japanese restaurant. It was then served at the table still breathing, all in the name of freshness. God would not have anything to do with blessing any of these horrors. I have also heard about the cutting off of the fins of live sharks and throwing the animals back into the ocean or the killing of dolphins and whales. And in many Asian cultures, they tie a snake upside down by its tail and skin it alive. Don't expect to be blessed—wake up! The only thing that these horrors do is cause you and your finances to be cursed.

There are so many more horrific examples that I could have included, but I'm positive you've gotten the point. It's no wonder that try as they may, these cultures and businesses just don't seem to get ahead any more than they are. Dare I say it—they're in bondage! Your finances are in bondage! It's these sins with animals that are the cause of a lot of their problems. These sins with animals have had these cultures and business for thousands of years in a stranglehold of spiritual bondages. It's all due to how they treat the animals of this earth. America is blessed far above other cultures because if you think about it, we do less live animal torture in the name of freshness or tradition with the animals that we eat. We have less inhumane treatment with the animals that are in our care than any other country. But America still needs to be at the forefront and show the rest of the world how to do it by making it the law that if you own any animal, then you must provide for it a seventy-five-degree environment that it can freely go in and out of.

There are still cultures that believe that the body parts of certain animals can heal them. This is so false it's not even funny. In China and Japan, they believe that the testicles of animals can heal you. Isaiah 53:5 says, *"And by His [Jesus's] stripes we are healed."* Jesus is your only healer, not the body parts of any animal in this world. This kind of wrong belief is breaking two of Gods commandments. The first one is called idolatry, sound familiar. I purposely quoted this Scripture again because it is the key to your success. You must turn away from all other false gods. There is only one true God, Jesus Christ. Exodus 20:3-6 says, *"You shall have no other gods before me."* The second commandment says:

> *You shall not make for yourself a carved image—any likeness of anything that is in heaven above or beneath, or that is in the water under the earth; you shall not bow down to them nor serve them. For I, the Lord your God, am a jealous God, visiting the iniquity of the fathers upon the children to the third and fourth generations of those who hate Me, but showing mercy to thousands, to those who love Me and keep My commandments.*

What God is saying is that if you put your focus on anything else to get your needs met or if you worship anything other than Jesus and His Word, then that's idolatry. If these cultures would drop all of these sinful traditions, wake up, put their focus on Jesus, and adopt God's laws and ways of doing things then they would find all these yokes, chains, and bondages would just start falling off their lives and cultures. A yoke is a spiritual term. It is anything in the spirit realm that has caused things in the natural realm to not work. For example, you gamble all the time and you can't stop. That's a yoke that has you in bondage. You can't see any other way to get money other than to gamble. We do nothing in our own power. That's why a spiritually mature Christian can use the name above all names, Jesus Christ of Nazareth, together with the wisdom of the Bible and obeying Jesus's laws. This will break the power of a yoke or a bondage that has erected itself in a person's life. But this does not mean that once the yoke or bondage has broken off of your life that you can ever go back into such an unrighteous lifestyle.

Philippians 4:19 says, *"And my God shall supply all your need according to His riches in glory by Christ Jesus."* Matthew 15:6 says, *"Thus you have made the commandment of God of no effect by your traditions."* God does not bless man's traditions; He blesses obedience to His Word. When I was in my late teens and I read Philippians 4:19 I immediately got a vision of Jesus standing in front of me, and I asked him for some money. And he only peeled off a one-dollar bill from a huge roll of money and handed it to me. I was so angry at that verse of Scripture. I didn't like Jesus having control of my money. I now know as a mature Christian a few decades later that, that thought came directly from a devil. Now that I have a close personal relationship with Jesus through His Word and the wisdom of the Holy Spirit that lives inside me, I also now know that Jesus is testing our obedience to His Word. He wants to dump by the truck full an abundance of wealth and blessings without measure onto all of us. Your **lack of knowledge** in His Word, so that you can use your faith to connect the natural with the supernatural is what stops God's blessings, not God. So get His wisdom. Your sinful acts toward the animals of this earth will hold you tight with spiritual chains, yokes, and bondages. It also opens the door to the supernatural realm letting the devil in to steal kill and destroy everything in your life.

The Holy Spirit has also been dealing with me about watching any animal being killed and fighting for its last breath while being attacked on TV. We should not look at such things. Our eyes are a gate to our minds. Our minds record and file away into our hearts these horrors. You are what you see and hear. God instructs us in His Word not to have our minds wide open but to strongly guard our eye gates and our ear gates. In the Garden of Eden, there was no death. It was alien to Adam and Eve. God never intended for human beings or the animals, for that matter, to know anything about death. The Holy Spirit's convictions has been so strong in me that when an animal is killing another animal or another person is killing another person on TV, I have to turn the channel quickly just to receive my peace back. As Christians, we must never have a hard and calloused heart. Being obedient when the Holy Spirit convicts you to turn that off is being very wise. In God's eyes, all animals are very important to Him.

And for all those people who paid thousands of dollars to have their pets cryogenically frozen, you can kiss your money good-bye. For those of you who do not know what cryogenics is, I will explain it to you in laymen's terms. Cryogenics is the study and use of low-temperature phenomena. The cryogenic temperature range is from -238° F and -150° C to absolute zero. Some people believe that when a dead human or animal is put into cryogenic chamber, they will be able to reanimate or in other words bring back to life that person or that animal at a later date. In other words, these people who do this believe that the animal or body part will be brought back to life in the future. Unfortunately, coming back to life in this manner cannot ever happen because the only way you will ever be able to see your pets or your human loved ones again is to be born again.

John 3:3 says, "*Jesus answered and said to him, 'Most assuredly. I say to you, unless one is born again, he cannot see the kingdom of God.'*" Ecclesiastes 12:7 says, "*And the dust returns to the ground it came from, and the spirit returns to God who gave it.*" Only the spirit of a born-again believer returns back to Jehovah God. When a person accepts Jesus as his or her King and Savior, the supernatural power of the Holy Spirit enters that person and brings to life that person's once damned spirit. This is what Christians refer to as being **born again** their spirit is now **saved** from eternal separation from Jesus. Or, in simpler terms the power of Jehovah God regenerates your once dead or perishable spirit and brings it back to life the moment a person accepts Jesus of Nazareth as Their Lord and Savior making it an imperishable spirit now able to enter heaven. Then at the appointed time, all the people with their **imperishable** new spirits will have their **perishable** bodies transformed in the twinkling of an eye into **imperishable** new bodies and raptured up to the third heaven to attend the wedding fest with Jesus of Nazareth. Second Samuel 12:23 says, "*Can I bring him back again? I will go to him one day, but he cannot return to me.*"

The Word of God says Second Corinthians 5:8 *to be absent from the body is to be present with the Lord.* King David is saying that he will die and go to heaven but that his son cannot come back to life to be with him right now in this present age. All animals have souls but they do not have spirits like human beings do. But they all do go to heaven. This also means all the animals that have become extinct or died will be resurrected again to live on the new earth on the eighth day, along with all the other planets that Christians will inhabit in the new age forever. So as born-again Christians, we will all be reunited with all of our pets; don't you worry.

But only Jesus Christ will have the power to resurrect all of the people who died without accepting Him as their Lord and savior. Now all of these people are at what is called their day of judgment. If anyone is saved and you have had an abortion and you have repented or if you've had any miscarriages, you will be united with those babies also. Halleluiah! If you're not saved and you had miscarriages or any abortions, your babies will still be living forever in heaven with Jesus. God is so good. Nothing falls through the cracks of this universe without God catching it.

CHAPTER 10

MAN'S BEST FRIEND?

In a wolf family, there are so many parallels to the human family. Except for one, not even wolf parents of a litter of eight-week-old puppies would give them up at eight weeks of age. But for some reason, we humans think that it's all right for us to tear that baby away from its mother at such a young age. Yes, I understand that this is another human custom, but would you do that with a human baby? I do understand that there are extenuating circumstances to every situation. The point that I am making is that puppies in the wild stay with their parents for two years or more, and some never leave. They stay in the family for life.

We also think that there's no crime in throwing that baby outside by itself into the backyard. Your backyard is only for your dog to go potty in. It's also to run around and play with you and get some exercise in. There's another thing that should be against the law, and that is to get a puppy or a dog or any animal that you will not be able to keep for the duration of its whole life. Human beings don't do this with their children; don't do this with animals. For example, if you're in the military and you know that you could be transferred to another base where you know that you will not be able to take this animal with you, then it is extremely irresponsible of you to even get an animal! Animals suffer emotional trauma and have abandonment issues just like people do, and many people overlook this fact.

Yes, in all animal families, unfortunate things do take place inside each family unit. We should also be ashamed of ourselves for what we have done to the domesticated dog. We've bestowed the grand title of man's best friend to only one animal in the whole world—our pet dogs. The horrible things that we have done to them makes me think, *Wow! If this is how we treat man's best friend, I'd hate to be man's worst friend.*

As a Christian I believe the Word of God, and it states that when an animal dies, its soul goes to heaven. If you have to have your pet put down, just remember that its next breath will be in the presence of Jesus.

God has dominion over all of mankind. I can also positively say to you that God is not sitting up in heaven and looking down on us and saying, "You dumb humans. You get what you deserve, or you just don't know any better. You're just a dumb human." Does this sound familiar? We say these things about the very animals that God has given us dominion over. I have personally heard people say words to this effect to or about animals. Yet God has dominion over us and He doesn't ever do that to us. We should not do it to what we've been given dominion over either.

Matthew 5:48 says, *"You must be perfect just as your father in heaven is perfect."* We are the animal kingdom's caretakers, not their jailers or abusers or torturers. The earth and all of its fullness is God's. He wants to reward us for taking care of what's His. That means the money is God's. Your spouse and your children are God's, and yes, all of the animal kingdom is God's. If you get an animal, you must be responsible by having it spayed or neutered.

And it's also a lie that letting your female dog have at least one litter of puppies will make her better tempered. It doesn't. The Humane Society will attest to this fact. Just because your dog is a purebred is not any reason to breed it. That's just plain irresponsible and selfish. We have more than enough purebred breeders in this world. We don't need this, nor does this world have the room for anymore. Being proud of yourself for being a responsible dog owner is a great feeling. It's better than being responsible for millions of homeless animals or for millions of animals that had to be euthanized because of overpopulation.

There are twelve million dogs in America alone that are put down each year according to the Humane Society. Do you really want to be responsible for that? Can you live and sleep at night with their blood on your hands? Good professional breeders will make sure to have new owners for the new babies before they ever breed their animals. They also will have very in-depth interviews with each prospective new owner. And contracts will be signed specifying that if anything happens and the new owner for whatever reason cannot care for or keep the animal any longer, then it must be returned to the breeder. This is a twenty-to-forty year lifestyle most of the time for these professional breeders. I know that I repeat myself, but trust me it is for a very good reason. I want all of this to drop down into your heart and for you to be forever changed by the revelations that you learn in this book. Sometimes their businesses have been passed down from generation to generation. We all know a lot more about animals in this day and age than ever before. But with all the injustices that we have inflicted on animals for thousands of years and now with all of our wisdom, when is it going to stop? When will we come into the light? When will we wake up?

CHAPTER 11

WOLVES!

In the wild, animals pass down instructions to each other from generation to generation, from how to hunt to how to hide from predators and so on. For example, a mating wolf pair will spend two years with the help of the whole wolf pack teaching the puppies everything that they will need to know to be a viable addition to the family unit. Each wolf pup will need to be taught how to pull its own weight in its first two years. The pups will be spoiled and played with by all and loved. They will also have a babysitter that will watch them and take care of them while the rest are on the hunt. This babysitter will have a babysitter in training, and both will fight to the death to protect the puppies in their care.

At two years of age, the pups graduate. They are now invited to go out onto the hunt. This is the equivalent of us going to work. Wolves spend ten to twelve hours on the hunt, and sometimes they will run for hours at a gallop running their prey into the ground. This is a lot different from running for hours on end versus our domesticated dogs who sit mostly for twenty-four hours each and everyday. And then we put food down on the floor for them. The most that they do is to wag their tails.

The A.K.C and mixed breed of dogs of today are all hybrids that came from the pure version that Jehovah God created which is the wolf. When wolves are on the hunt their body temperature is like a raging hot furnace.

The domesticated dog's resting body temperature is only two degrees higher than that of a human's. So to leave a dog outside or any animal, for that fact, in any temperature that you yourself can't endure is torture and animal cruelty and ungodly. This includes all domesticated and wild animals that are your responsibility.

Did you know that cold or hot temperatures were used as high forms of torture to extract information from prisoners of war. If we human beings leave an animal that's in our care or we know of an animal in need and you have the means to bring that animal inside and care for its needs and you don't, then God holds you accountable, and now you're in sin.

Tell me, what crimes did the animals of this earth do to deserve a life filled each and everyday with pain of cold or hot weather? I've heard people say, "Oh, the animals like being outside. They have always been outside. They're used to it." No they aren't used to it. They didn't let sin in, but they sure have been forced to endure it. No human, animal, or plant was created to live in anything other than the Garden of Eden temperature. There is a Grand Canyon-sized difference between having a choice versus being forced into something.

Do a test. Build a huge barn or a heated house where your animals have the freedom to come and go and then put them inside this seventy-five-degree acclimatized structure. Then sit back and observe. Yes, they will venture outside to play just like you or I would. But when they get too cold or it's too uncomfortable for them, they will come back inside to warm up. Now there are some animals that just don't know any better, so you will have to do it for them and bring them inside. God did this with the Garden. Your animals' actions and body language will scream to you volumes on how to better care for their needs through this. I guarantee that you will learn a lot about your animals. Your animals have been trained to the old way of doing things, so now through repetition you can show them the right way.

This whole earth was forced into this weather. It was the plants and animals that were just left outside, but we humans made sure to take care of ourselves, didn't we? We built homes, malls, and office buildings with a set temperature inside them. And it's just like the Garden of Eden climate of seventy-five degrees. Now how funny is that? It's no coincidence that we set the temperature to seventy-five degrees, give or take a couple of degrees. It is the universal temperature that we human beings like to dwell in when we have the freedom of choice. We all agree that we are comfortable at seventy-five degrees. You might say, "Who says so?" Well, God says so with His example. It's the Garden of Eden.

I've also heard people say, "Well the earth has had this bad weather for thousands of years, and this is the way it's supposed to be. It's always been like this." God set the earth's temperature in the Garden of Eden at seventy-five degrees. How do I know this? Because when God made the Garden of Eden, He created it to meet all of our needs with nothing lacking. It was perfect. It was paradise. This includes a comfortable climate to live and exist in forever. He knew the exact temperature that all the plants and animals and human beings would need to thrive in. It was the entrance of sin into this realm that moved it out of position, along with everything else.

There is another huge piece of wisdom that is found inside the Lord's Prayer Jesus instructs us on how we should pray. This prayer reveals God's desire for the way it is in heaven to be just like that here on earth. This is the part of the Lords' prayer that I'm talking about. It reads, "*Thy will be done here on earth as it is in heaven.*" Heaven is a comfortable seventy-five degrees or we would be very uncomfortable or dead from the wrong temperature. That's why many of the plants and animals, along with millions of people, are dying here on this earth from deadly temperatures. Luke 11:2 says:

> *Our father who art in heaven hollowed be thy name thy kingdom come thy will be done here on earth as it is in heaven give us this day our daily bread and forgive us our trespasses as we forgive those who have trespassed against us and lead us not into temptation but deliver us from evil for yours is the kingdom and the power and the glory in Jesus Christ name amen.*

In this prayer Jesus is telling us that we are to pray for the exact way it is in heaven to be manifested here on earth. That includes heaven's climate to be the same here on earth. What do you think heaven's temperature is? Never thought about before, have you? This prayer is more proof that even Jesus does not approve of this temperature, this climate, or this weather. We cannot change this weather here on earth, but what we can do is to bring all the animals that we care for and own into acclimatized barns and dwelling quarters. Because of the money that you spend on these acclimatized habitats, God will open the heavens and pour you out blessings that you will not have room to receive. But God can't bless you when you are not caring for His animals the way He has shown you to. This is where you step out in faith and trust God's Word that says when you get sin out of your life He will now be able to bless you.

You see, this kind sin has been right under our noses ever since the fall of man. We just never saw it. It comes along with a lot of chains, yokes, and bondages. That sin is what has been keeping you from ever getting ahead. It's held you back and kept you down. Change this and bring all your animals inside. Then watch how you prosper. Watch your life finally blossom because now your finances have been loosed.

Chapter 12

Training People First

There are many people who have no business having animals at all, ever. It's just like when you and I can look at someone's kid and tell just how smart or stupid their parents are about parenting. I can also look at a dog or any pet and tell just how educated the owner is about animals just by how the animal behaves. You see, your children and your pets are the sum amount of what you teach or don't teach them. One example is that I have taught my dogs that they are not allowed to bark outside. If they hear someone outside trying to break in, then yes. I taught them that whenever I let them outside. I always had one eye on them so that I could see if anyone was trying to steal them or hurt them. Then there are dog owners who do not know how to teach their dogs anything, and it shows.

One day I was walking my show dog, a Harlequin Great Dane, down the street. We came up to a yard with four attention-starved black dogs in it, which I knew about because I had driven past this same house many times before in my car and had noticed that they were always outside abandoned to solitary confinement in the backyard. As we neared the yard, they rushed the fence and assaulted us with their barking. Excalibur and I just stood there looking at these four monsters going crazy. I leaned towards them and said, "You guy's need a new mommy and daddy, don't you". Those poor dogs didn't stop for one breath. As I walked away I felt very sorry for them and I later called the Police on base, we were in the Air Force at that time.

Now if you were to walk past my house and Excalibur was standing next to the chain link fence in our back yard, you would be able to walk by in peace. First, if my dog is outside, someone is supervising him. We are either outside with him or someone is watching him through an open window. Second, when no one is home, he's in our house, so he stay's warm in the winter and cool in the summer. That's being a responsible dog owner. Ever since Excalibur was nine weeks old, he's been on a potty routine. As an adult, he now goes out to go potty every three and a half hours like clockwork. Yes, there were many times I had to get up in the middle of the night because I did not have a doggie door. If he had to go potty, he would lay his big head on my chest to wake me up to take him out. He had me trained very well.

Third, anyone who lets their dogs charge and bark at people like that should not have them. That's so irresponsible. As a dog owner, your dog's barking abuses your neighbors. They don't want to hear your dog's barking. Your neighbors do not live at the dog pound. You're using your dogs barking as an audible weapon, and so you're beating up your neighbors with your dog's noise pollution! Look, if you need protection, get an alarm system. They're dirt cheap!

When you have an animal in your care, God expects a lot out of you. You'll be doing yourself a favor and very wise to put all your animals on set routines as soon as possible. If your animals know what's going to happen next and when, it alleviates a lot of restless behavior and anxieties in your animals. Your animal will have to go to the bathroom many, many times each day. People ask me if they should get an animal. I ask them, "Do you like poop?" The reason is because that's what you will be cleaning up 99 percent of the time.

Depending on the animal, they will go at least once an hour. Now if you trained them to hold it for three and a half hours, that's all right, but no longer. To force an animal to hold it for more than three and a half hours is not only animal cruelty, but it also permanently damages their bladder. It stretches it, and that's why your dog piddles all over the place. It has no muscle control now. It's just like when you sneeze and then you pee all over yourself. When you were younger, for whatever reason, you had that first urge to go pee and you didn't. You just held it. Now that you're older, because of that you have stretched your own bladder and now you have no muscle control either. The only difference with that is that you caused your dog's body to be damaged. The dog didn't do that to itself.

With my large dogs I found that you should plan to stay home for the first year to teach them how to live in the house with you. And six months with your smaller dogs. I would first start and leave for five minutes. Then after a few times of that, I would leave for ten minutes. After that a few times, I would increase the length of time that I was gone. All the time you are programming them. Their minds are a blank tape. They are what you create them to be.

I was taught by watching my Great Dane's body language that if I came home after three and a half hours, his body language told me that was just too long. How do I know? Because as soon as I opened the front door, he said hello to me and then raced to the back door to be let out. I started making sure that I always came back before three and a half hours or I made sure that someone was there on the dot to let him out. I found out that at three and a half hours, I would come in the door and he would spend a lot of time greeting me in the living room. Then I would walk him slowly to the back door to go out and to go potty. Only this time he wasn't as anxious and excited as he was before when he had to wait longer to go potty. If you're not trying to accommodate your animals, you're failing to give them a quality lifestyle. If you really love them then give them to someone who can figure out what works for them.

Here's what I did. You might want to try this potty arrangement. It worked out very well for me. I had three phone numbers on my calendar next to the kitchen phone. I would call the night before and ask for whoever was available for the following day. If I was going to be gone longer than three and a half hours, I then asked them to please let him out at two specific times and so on. At the end of the month, we would all add up each of our records of the dates and times that we had saved. Then we compared notes, and I paid each person two dollars for each time they let my dog out.

At that time, with that dog, I was a manicurist, so I bartered with them for fills or pedicures and full sets of nails. It always worked out, and we all were very happy, even the dog. The point here is to pay whoever comes over to let your dogs out. You see, if someone tells you that they'll take care of your dog or let your dog out for free, they won't take it seriously, but when you're talking money, now you've got their attention. Through repetition, your animals will learn this routine. It's something that should continue for the rest of your pets life.

There are some animals that don't really care. It is not that important to them what's next. There are other animals that go crazy not knowing what's going on or what's going to happen next. Consider an animal taken out of an unstable home where everything in its life was unsure or crazy. That same neurotic animal will blossom in a calm and structured home with a loving, secure routine that it can count on for the rest of its life. Most of the time animals use their body movements as their language to communicate to each other.

As another example, I was to leave for a church retreat for the weekend, and I was going over some last-minute details with my husband about how to take care of our two dogs. I told my husband that when Excalibur wants water, he will hang his head over the kitchen sink. He likes cold running water. And when he is hungry, he will sit in front of the refrigerator. When he wants to go potty, he will sit in front of the back door. My husband said that he did not know that Excalibur did all of this because he does not do these things for him. I said, "You see, even the dog is smart enough to know that you do not understand his body language, and so he does not even bother to do it for you." Animals are very smart. In retrospect, I now know I made a horrible mistake trusting my husband with those dogs. Animals, being highly visual creatures, not only read each other's body language, but they also read a human's body language.

They talk to us or to each other with a growl, a bark, a howl, and so on. They're communicating their wants and desires to us and to each other when they are mad, scared, or afraid or they just want to come in or outside. They will use their audible voice and their body language to let us know. Please don't ignore your animals when they're screaming at you with their body language. It's your job to learn to communicate with your animal by watching your animal's body language or audible voice or at least trying to learn and understand what it is saying to you. If you don't, how can you ever consider yourself a good owner, and how can you ever get their needs met? Please stop and see what your animals really saying to you with their bodies and their voices because they are screaming at you with their actions loud and clear. I just hope for their sake you really see it.

Let's start with an eight-week-old puppy. The first thing you should teach it is the word potty and the word no. In the first week, you can tell if they have picked up those two words. Each animal learns at its own pace. You will see this kind of light go off in their eyes like, "Okay, I understand that." Let your animal baby sleep with you for the first few weeks. Now I'm not talking about birds or hoofed animals. You must use your own discretion. But like with all babies, there will be a few months where you're not going to be getting a full night's sleep. You have time on your side because in a few months they will have matured and learned.

Use this first year wisely. You must put time into them. You must be there, because everything you teach them will pay off for you in the future. After getting up many times in the night and carrying your baby outside and watching to see with you own eyes that it did indeed go potty. If you can, in a few weeks, you will know when, move it down into its own bed on the floor. You're still going to sleep light and getting up when you get that cold nose to take them out unless you have a doggie door. Never break this repetition. You are training your animal with repetition to do just what you expect. Use repetition for the rest of your animal's life to teach it whatever you want it to do.

If you do not have a doggie door, then the success of teaching your animal how to get you to let it out is all up to you. This is one of the many reasons why you need to be home for the first year. Walls can't teach your animals anything. I don't believe in crating an animal while in your house is right. That's just animal cruelty. I can understand it for short drives in your car for the animal's safety, but do not crate an animal just because you want it out of your way so you don't have to deal with it. That's a living creature. You are a living creature. Wake up!

A large litter box is a great idea for smaller dogs if there is a place for you to put the box. Also, there is a flushable cat box. It hooks up to your water source in the bathroom or next to the laundry water source. Dogs or cats, it does not matter. It's number one and number two. It's called the Cat Genie. It costs $350, but it's so worth it. It's easy to install, and best of all, you don't ever have to clean the box because it flushes itself either into the toilet or into your laundry water drain. Halleluiah, we have been set free.

If you have door training, this is a serious trust issue between you and your pet, which you cannot break. If they go potty in your house, it's your fault, not theirs. And never put your pet outside to punish it for going potty inside. This is just digging you an even deeper grave, so to speak. You're only teaching your pet it would rather get spanked for going potty inside than to be left outside in either the freezing cold or the choking heat. When your pet sits at the door while you're home, this is your pet's body language saying, "I have to go outside *now!*" And vice versa—as soon as it sits at the door to come in, you must immediately let it inside. Do not let it wait.

When you take an animal as your own, guess what? You are now the animal's slave. That's right. They're not wild; they are domesticated. It's like serving an invalid old person for the rest of his or her life. So while you're home with your baby pet, you must never let it out of your sight. This way you will see the, "I've got to go potty" signs. You're blessed because babies sleep all the time. The only reasons they wake up are: 1.) To go to the bathroom. 2.) To eat or drink. 3.) To play. For the first six months, pets are very needy. Thankfully they are growing up, and it won't be like this forever. As soon as you see them sniffing around, pick them up and take them outside. If at that time they only went pee, then be on the lookout for the poo; it's to be expected in the next twenty minutes or so. As your pet gets older and as each day and each week passes, use your time home to teach it everything it will need to know to live in your home. You planned to stay home for your human baby; you must also plan to stay home for your pet baby. Again, the circumstances are different for every animal baby.

An animal should never ever be an impulse buy. This is to be taken as seriously as having a human baby. Now after you have spent two years raising and training let's just say a couple dogs. Then this is a good time to start having your own children. This order of dogs first and then children is smarter. After your human baby comes home from the hospital, do not separate your dogs from the family unit or the newborn baby. Your newborn child does not know the difference right now but the dogs do. As *the alpha male and female* of your family, you need to let the dogs know that this is their new brother or sister, figuratively speaking, and that they have nothing to be jealous about.

You should lavish lots of affection on the dogs right now as long as they are respectful to the new addition to the family. Always, always supervise at all times when children and animals are together. This is for both the animal and the child's protection. Some children, when you are not looking, will hurt an animal on purpose. You also don't want dogs to be jealous of each other or your human baby. Animals are very visual creatures. I always petted both my dogs at the same time and fed them at the same time. Do not play favorites. This is very dangerous. Don't do it with your animals, and don't do it with your children. Now we all know that your children are more important than your animals, but the animal must be taught that it is second and your children are first. Another thing that helps with the door training should be done at about eight or nine months, and again it depends on the breed of animal. If I have to work the next day, I will stop the water that they drink at seven or eight o'clock at night. I have found that doing this and letting them outside to go potty just before I go to bed makes a huge difference. They will usually not have to go potty as much in the middle of the night.

Then you must bathe your pet. After all, you live in the house and you take a bath every day. Your dog should be on a bath routine once a week a cat every six months, if needed. Start your animals' bathing routines when they're young. This is the best way to get them used to having a bath.

Give each pet its own chew toy. They shouldn't have to share. This will cause jealousy between them and fights. But if they're anything like my dogs, they will want to take the other's toy just to make him chase after him. Wherever you go, always bring their toys with them. Their toys give them something to do. Dogs get a great deal of pleasure just chewing away on a toy or a chew bone. It releases a lot of anxiety. Better the toy than you or your furniture.

Now I'm not talking about aggressive and dangerous behavior. You must address that at the start and defuse it at once. In a case of aggressive behavior when an animal is young, tell the animal no with a stern tone in your voice. With an older dog, if you know this dog is not a biter, then do the same stern no repeatedly. The animal will soon realize that this is not acceptable behavior. Nip it in the butt. Unacceptable behavior not addressed will spiral out of control. Call in an expert if you have a biter or a nipper that has gotten out of control.

All nipping and biting is a fear-based behavior. If you know that the nipping or biting has extenuating circumstances and you know the cause, such as you saw children teasing or hurting the animal, tell the children that you do not treat animals in that way and if they are caught doing it again then they will be reprimanded. Then tell the animal no once, but if the animal bites or nips again unprovoked, a spanking a couple times on the behind never hurt anyone. A fly swatter really stings. One swat from that and the next time all you have to do is to look like you're just reaching for it and they get the message. I say a fly swatter never killed anything but a fly or spiders, and to a dog, once on the butt is all it takes. They get the message loud and clear.

For all zoos and shelters that house animals, the floors should be heated in the winter and a soft bed that is at least one foot off the ground must be provided for each animal with access to a 75 degree environment at all times. Also, a warm pool along with the cool water pool needs to be installed. The hot water will alleviate any pain that an animal may be experiencing. You will be surprised at how often the warm pool in the winter gets used and the cool pool gets used in the summer. For family pets that have stuffed beds that are on the floor, put a plastic tarp under it, the kind that you put under your sleeping bag when you go camping. This will stop the crippling cold air from coming up through the concrete and the rug into your house and into your pet's body while it sleeps.

I know about this cold air coming up through the floor of my new home first hand. I didn't have a bed yet, so I made my bed on the floor in my bedroom. The next morning when I woke up, I couldn't move. One of my lungs was so cold and stiff that I could hardly take in a breath. I almost thought that I would have to go to the emergency room. The pain was unbelievable, but I had to go to work. As I got ready, I went and called the prayer line and rebuked this attack against my body. I went to work in pain, but as the day progressed, the pain finally left and I was able to breathe.

Human beings have flesh, muscle, and bone just like animals have. In this respect, we are no different. The Lord told me that as I was writhing in pain that morning. He also said, "Animals are not impervious to pain. They feel the same pains that humans feel, so what is uncomfortable for you is just as uncomfortable for animals." The Lord told me that people must stop saying and thinking, "*Oh, it's just an animal. It doesn't feel any pain or it doesn't care.*" That's a lie straight from hell.

CHAPTER 13

BAD PEOPLE HAPPEN TO GOOD ANIMALS

All your dog really wants after living its entire life by your side and giving you all its love and faithfulness is to die peacefully in your arms, looking into the eyes of the one that it loved its whole life; that's you, and that includes the pit bull breed.

If people put their minds to it, they could train any breed of dog to be vicious and to fight. Unfortunately, some ungodly people just happened to have picked the wonderful **Staffordshire Terrier**, also known by its slang name as, the **Pit Bull Terrier**.

People give pit bulls a bad rap by training them to be mean. These lovely, sweet dogs were fine when they were born, and then a bad person happened to them. When a pit bull or any dog mauls or kills, it's the dog that did the crime who is also a victim because now it must pay the high price of being put down. I believe all the blame has to go to the person who trained and tortured the animal for this bad behavior to come out of this breed. That person must be punished for the people or other animals that were attacked or even killed. That person's punishment needs to be heavy. It must send out a message. Pit bulls are not born that way. These people will be punished for ruining this breed and any animal.

I have also personally seen an animal hurt or mistreat a person or another animal, and it's soon after that I see that same animal get it back, only worse. I have seen innocent people and animals have bad things happen to them. That's due to the sinful world that we live in. As Christians, we all know that we don't have to do anything wrong to another person for him or her to dislike us or to attack us. We know that demons possess and use these people.

Proverbs 27:19 says, *"People may think that they are doing what is right, but the Lord examines the, heart."* Thank God that He judges men's hearts. This way nothing is hidden from the eyes of God. Psalm 94:11 says, *"The Lord knows the thoughts of man."* Luke 6:38 says, *"For with the same measure that you use, it will be measured back to you."* That means man and animals receive a harvest of blessings or curses. Nothing goes unpunished here or unrewarded. Even the animals get their recompense here on earth. Are you shocked to hear that even an animal will receive a good or bad harvest for its actions? Why do you believe it when an unbeliever says that he or she is receiving his or her karma for what they have done? Think about it.

But to all the animal lovers from around the world who had to endure the pain of seeing or hearing about the abuse of an innocent animal, You can breathe a huge sigh of relief because their abusers will be punished in the here and now for their crimes against animals. Wow, the more I learn about my Jesus, the more in love I am with Him.

That reminds me of when I was in one of those helpless situations. I heard about a little puppy that was being abused. I was working at this place, and the owner was a heathen, she and her whole family. Also, all of my coworkers were not saved, and they all totally despised and mocked me at every turn. I knew that it was because I was the only Christian at my job, but I couldn't leave. I needed the money, and because of the circumstances I was in, I endured. I was like a piece of coal. I was trapped on all sides. During those six years of hell, God turned that piece of coal into a diamond.

I learned more about spiritual warfare during those six years than in any other time in my life. On one of the many days that I had been crying out to God, I asked Him why He put me there. I'll never forget what He said to me: *"I put a light in a dark place."* So in return for all of my coworkers' and clients' attacks, I prayed for all their salvations every day. When any of them needed prayer or someone's shoulder to cry on, guess who they came to? That's right, me.

Now back to the animal abuse that I had to hear about. The owner was a single parent who was always too busy looking for a man. She had no time for her own five children, which are from four different fathers. And still she thought that she could find love by getting a small toy bred puppy to put her affections on. This made her youngest child, who was a very hefty five-year-old, even more jealous. Now guess who this five-year-old boy would take his anger out on? You got it, that innocent little puppy. He would torture and terrorize this puppy. The owner knew that hearing about this would upset me, so she would come into work and tell all these horrible stories.

She laughed at how her child had dropkicked this puppy and had knocked it unconscious. I needed my job desperately, and I knew if I called the police, that she would have known it was me. Plus, I had seen God's power fix problems not only in my life but also in the lives of the people I have prayed for in the past in remarkable ways. Every day I called the *700 Club* and TBN, and I kept prayer for that puppy's freedom and protection on their prayer chapels. There was another time she came into work and told us that she had to take the twelve-week-old puppy to the vet. Its x-rays showed that it had a broken leg, and now it had a cast on its little leg. Every day I was so mad and I felt so helpless on how to save this little puppy. I prayed and prayed that God would remove this puppy from this family.

Then about a month later, the owner came into work and told all of us that she had a desire to sell the puppy for $300. When I heard that I was so happy, but I still held my breath until that puppy was out of that hell hole. Then the day came, and I heard those wonderful words. The owner came in and told us that she had sold the puppy to an elderly couple. Alleluia! I was so happy and relieved that God had answered my prayers. Then I asked God, "Now what's going to happen to this little boy because of all the evil that he did to this little puppy." The Lord just told me to wait and watch. He also reminded me of the Scriptures about seedtime and harvest and how in due season we all shall reap whatsoever we sow. I felt as if the Lord wanted me to see something here in the supernatural realm. I learned that when I got onto God's timeline. I then started to see how God's laws came to pass in the different situations that I was in. It's like, "Wow all this has been going on all along and I've never seen it like this before." I'm watching with my spiritual eyes, and I'm ever so sensitive to everything and my surroundings. Now I'm seeing things that used to just fly past me. This is what the Word of God does to you. It's like someone has just turned on the lights, only it's not in a room. It's the whole world.

About three months went by. A season is about three or four months. Depending on what you're going through, it could be longer. The owner was always on the phone with her child's school. In her conversations, I gathered that her child was having nightmares and couldn't sleep at all. He was also too afraid to go to school because the other children at school were beating him up and bullying him. They were kicking him, pulling his hair, and tormenting him. I also heard that he was pushed down three stairs and was knocked unconscious. Another time he fell or was pushed and broke his arm. It was now in a cast. All this information might not all be in the exact order of events, and I don't really know if all his injuries happened at school, but this was everything that happened to her son.

I heard everything that he did to that puppy, and in due season, I also heard how it all came back on this boy and then some. I realized that when God's laws are broken, even by a five-year-old child, they will still manifest in the lives of those who operate them, no matter how young or old they are. I heard it all unfold before me. It took about five or six months. I lived it. I felt sorry for that little boy, but it was his mother's fault. She's too busy to read and teach her children the Bible. All the answers are all in there. It tells you just how this world works. I give all the glory to God, who sent His angels to move that puppy out of there. Galatians 6:7–8 says, *"Do not be deceived, God is not mocked; for whatever a man sows, that he will also reap. For he who sows to his flesh will of the flesh reap corruption, but he who sows to the Spirit will of the Spirit reap everlasting life."*

This goes for cock fighting or forcing any animals to fight for whatever reasons. This is not from God. He's never going to bless this mess. If anything, all the death seeds that you are sown into your life by fighting these animals will multiply quickly against you and overtake and drag you down to utter destruction. So please stop now. Stop sinning, and just let all the death seeds that you have sown into your life already just die out after a few months. Keep doing good and I promise the roses in your life will begin to bloom again. God is such a good God. He's not mad at you. He loves you so much, and He's on your side. But if you get yourself out into sin, then you have made yourself fair game for the demons.

Now if you ever decide to get a dog, do yourself a favor and get two puppies. Let them choose each other not for breeding but as lifelong companions for each other. As a human, you can't give your dogs what another dog can. And you would never give a human baby to a child. Then do not give a child an animal or animal baby and expect the child to care for the needs of this animal. If a responsible adult is taking care of all the needs of the animal and there is a child or a young adult there, always supervise them. I'm praying for stronger laws concerning who is allowed to own animals.

CHAPTER 14

AN ANGEL OF GOD DID IT!

I used to love to watch those shows on TV where animals would rescue or save the lives of people. News flash—the Holy Spirit came in the form of a dove when Jesus was baptized, and He can also use animals to save the life of a person. Here is just one example of an angel of the Lord communicating to a donkey not to go any farther. The Holy Spirit used an angel to cause Balaam's donkey to stop and to rebuke Balaam with a human voice and saved Balaam's life. Numbers 22:28–33 says:

> *Then the lord caused the donkey to speak. "What have I done to you that deserves your beating me these three times?" It asked Balaam. "Because you have made me to look like a fool! If I had a sword with me I would kill you!" "But I am the same donkey that you ride on," the donkey answered. "Have I done anything like this before?" "No," he admitted. Then the Lord opened Balaam's eyes, and he saw the angel of the Lord standing in the roadway with a drawn sword in his hand. Balaam fell down on the ground before him. "Why did you beat your donkey those three times?" the angel of the Lord demanded. "I have come to block your way because you are stubbornly resisting me. Three times the donkey saw me*

and shied away; otherwise, I would certainly have killed you by now and spared the donkey."

First Kings 17:4–6 says, *"Drink from the brook and eat what the ravens bring you, for I have commanded them to bring you food. So Elijah did as the Lord had told him and camped beside Kerith Brook. The ravens brought him bread and meat each morning and evening, and he drank from the brook."*

These Scriptures prove that the Holy Spirit uses the angels of God to move animals to do heroic acts. I just want to see people give Jehovah God His just due credit for saving all these people and animals. Likewise demons and evil spirits enter or oppress animals to do things. One account a true story were three maneless Lions of **Tsavo** who killed around a hundred people in eastern Africa in **1898.** A movie was made about these demonically oppressed male Lions in **1996.** The main horror of what these three lions did was that they did not kill because they were hungry and their target that they killed at this time where only humans. Genesis 3:1–5 says:

> *Now the serpent was more cunning than any beast of the field which the Lord God had made. And he [the devil in the serpent] said to the woman, "Has God indeed said, 'you shall not eat of every tree of the garden'?" And the woman said to the serpent, "We may eat the fruit of the trees of the garden; but of the fruit of the tree which is in the midst of the garden, God has said, 'you shall not eat it, nor shall you touch it, lest you die.'" Then the serpent said to the woman, "You will not surely die. For God knows that in the day you eat of it your eyes will be opened and you will be like God, knowing good and evil."*

Genesis 3:13 says, *"And the Lord God said to the woman, 'What is this you have done?' The woman said, 'The serpent deceived me, and I ate.'"* I also saw on television where people were talking about animals that could predict a person's death. Be careful because demon's get inside of animals, i.e. the serpent in the Garden of Eden. Demons will use an animal to lure a person into the occult or away from Jesus of Nazareth. Just test the spirit. So, the next time you see an animal go and lay in the bed of a person to let you know that their death is near, if that person is conscious, start leading him or her to the Lord and getting him or her saved. I guarantee you that animal will stop letting anyone know when someone is about to die ever again. How do I know this? Because if you're going to lead everyone to the Lord that an animal has revealed is going to die soon, then the devil's sure not going to let you know that anymore. He'll stop. The devil doesn't want anyone saved, so he will stop having that animal do that. And on the other hand if an angel of Jehovah God uses an animal to reveal to you when a person is about to die. Then yes use this animals signal to witness to that person.

Please don't have anything to do with these stinking familiar spirits. They're straight from the devil. A familiar spirit is another word for demonic spirit, such as a lying, cheating, stealing, drug, alcohol, sexually perverted spirits, and idolatry spirits. This is not a game. They're trying to kill you. They're very dangerous. They use anything to draw your attention away from God. The Bible tells us to have nothing to do with familiar spirits. It's a demonic spirit that's trying to lure you into getting your focus onto them. Demon possession is not always like it was in the movie *The Exorcist*. These demons hide inside people and inside of animals. Whenever a person or/and animal does anything good, it's the Holy Spirit or an angel of Jehovah God that caused them to do it. All good comes from the Lord, and all bad comes from the devil, so we know that all the glory goes to God through Jesus Christ alone. It was the Holy Spirit who did the miracles and all those great things, and yet all the credit went to the animals. That's so wrong. What's up with that?

The point that I'm trying to get you to see is that the Holy Spirit works through animals just like in the Bible when God used the whale to hold Jonah for three days. Demons have minimal powers, and they also use animals. They will do things to get you to put your faith and worship into them, so you need to know the Bible to not fall into any of their traps.

CHAPTER 15

THIS IS A WORLD WITHOUT END ...

One Hundred and twenty times throughout the Bible it states for a fact that this is a world without end. Here are just a couple of Scriptures KJV Eph. 3:21 & Isaiah 45:17. I thought I'd give you all a break and not *quote all one hundred and twenty Scripture's*. There will also be great tribulations leading up to the return of Jesus Christ.

Matthew 24:6

> *And wars will break out near and far, but don't panic yes, these things must come, but the end won't follow immediately. The nations and kingdoms will proclaim war against each other, and there will be famines and earthquakes in many parts of the world. But all this will be only the beginning of the horrors to come.*

Matthew 24:29 –31 says:

> *Immediately after those horrible days end, the sun will be darkened, the moon will not give light, the stars will fall from the sky, and the powers of heaven will be shaken. And then*

at last, the sign of the coming of the son of man that's [Jesus] will appear in the heavens, and there will be deep mourning among all the nations of the earth. And they will see the son of man [Jesus] arrive on the clouds of heaven with power and great glory. And He [Jesus] will send forth his angels with the sound of a mighty trumpet blast, and they will gather together his chosen ones [that's all the Christians] from the farthest ends of the earth and heaven.

Revelation 19:11 says, *"Then I saw a great white throne and Him [Jesus] who sat on it, from who's face the earth and the heaven fled away. And there was found no place for them."* It is because of God's great mercy that we are not consumed daily. Second Peter 3:8 NIV says, *"With the Lord a day is like a thousand years, and a thousand years are like a day."* So to Jehovah God He's given mankind seven days to repent. To mankind it's seven thousand years to repent. Personally, I think that's more than enough time to wait for all of us to repent. Don't you?

And for all those people who are trying to save the whales or the tigers or the giant pandas, they don't need saving. The animals that have gone to heaven are just fine and well with Jesus, waiting to repopulate the renewed earth in the new age.

I understand your hearts. I know where you are coming from, but you need to take the time to read the Bible, I'm talking every single word, the whole book ten times. You can read it once a year, you know.

I have to tell you this because if Jesus were here, he also would tell you. In fact, he already has. It's in the Bible.

Jesus would tell you that you are wasting valuable time and money when you could be busy with the people who are living and who need to be saved.

Jesus said Luke 9:60, *"Let the dead bury their own dead, but you go and proclaim the kingdom of God."* Jesus is talking about the more important things that are at hand, such as the salvation of billions of people before his return, the extinct animals, or the animals that are about to be extinct. They are all safe.

They, along with all the dinosaurs and every other plant or animal that has ever come to extinction, will all be resurrected to live forever in the renewed earth. You have Jesus of Nazareth's word on it!

I think the devil has had you sidetracked for way too long.

CHAPTER 16

JESUS CHRIST OF NAZARETH'S TRIUMPHANT RETURN!

Once in awhile I like to know what the world is saying. Here is one of their hypotheses on a secular TV station that caught my eye for a second or two. They're talking about what the world would be like without people on it. Now to me this is a very funny idea because of the mere fact that if they had only stopped to read the Bible, they would know that the only reason that the earth was even created was for human beings to live, as described in Genesis 1:27–31.

Thank God this world will always be inhabited by humans, but before that happens, Jesus will judge the wicked and the just, dividing the wheat from the tares, and give this beat-up earth a major facelift.

I give you Revelation 20:11–15, which says:

> *Then I saw a great white throne and Him who sat on it, from whose face the earth and the heaven fled away. And there was found no place for them. And I saw the dead [the unsaved], small and great, standing before God, and books were opened. And another book was opened, which is The Book of Life. And the dead [the unsaved] were judged according to their works, by the things which were written in*

the books. The sea gave up the dead [the unsaved] who were
in it, and Death and Hades delivered up the dead [unsaved]
who were in them. And they were judged, each one according
to his works. Then Death and Hades were cast into the lake
of fire.

Revelation 21:1–7 says:

Now I saw a new heaven and a new earth, for the first
heaven and the first earth had passed away. Also there was
no more sea. Then I, John, saw the holy city, New Jerusalem,
coming down out of heaven from God, prepared as a bride
adorned for her husband. And I heard a loud voice from
heaven saying, "Behold, the tabernacle of God is with men,
and He will dwell with them, and they shall be His people.
God Himself will be with them and be their God. "And God
will wipe away every tear from their eyes; there shall be no
more death, nor sorrow, nor crying. There shall be no more
pain for the former things have passed away." Then He [Jesus]
who sat on the throne said, "Behold, I make all things new."
And He said to me, "Write, for these words are true and
faith full." And He said to me, "It is done! I am the Alpha
and the Omega, the Beginning and the end. I will give of
the fountain of the water of life freely to him who thirsts." He
who overcomes shall inherit all things, and I will be his God
and he shall be my son.

Jesus, and only Jesus, will cause this old earth and heaven to pass
away before His face. The saved will be living with Him on the new earth
and new heaven that He creates for us. Nothing will ever stop that from
happening, thus fulfilling the prophecy spoken in the Bible that says in
Psalm 25:8, *"The meek shall inherit the earth."* Praise the Lord. Amen. His
return is very, very close now. I can't wait to see Jesus face to face. I'm
crying as I write this. Wow! I need to use this Scripture to make yet another
point. Second Peter 3:8 says *"With the Lord a day is like a thousand years,*

and a thousand years are like a day." God created the heavens and the earth in seven days. That's seven thousand years to us and only seven days to God. God does things in sevens, so starting from the seventh day on which God rested, Jesus will be returning sometime in the seven thousandth year from that day. Let me describe where we are in this seven thousand–year space of time. I'll use a clock as an example. Let's say that hypothetically 7:00 a.m. is when Jesus is scheduled to return to earth. Then right now in the year 2011, it's 6:55 a.m. That's five minutes before Jesus returns. We are there! This next Scripture happens at the end of the seven year tribulation. Revelation 19:11–21 says:

> *Then I saw heaven opened, and a white horse was standing there. And the one [Jesus] sitting on the horse was named Faithful and True for He judges fairly and then goes to war. His eyes were bright like flames of fire, and on his head were many crowns. A name was written on him, and only he knew what it meant. He was clothed with a robe dipped in blood, and his title was the Word of God. The armies of heaven, dressed in pure white linen, followed him on white horses. From His mouth came a sharp sword, and with it he struck down the nations. He ruled them with an iron rod, and he trod the winepress of the fierce wrath of almighty God. On his robe and thigh was written this title: King of kings and Lord of lords. Then I saw an angel standing in the sun, shouting to the vultures flying high in the sky. "Come! Gather together for the great banquet God has prepared. Come and eat the flesh of kings, captains, and strong warriors; of horses and their riders; and all humanity, both free and slave, small and great." Then I saw the beast gathering the kings of the earth and their armies in order to fight against the one sitting on the horse and his army. And the beast was captured, and with him the false prophet who did mighty miracles on behalf of the beast—miracles that had deceived all who had accepted the mark of the beast and who worshiped his statue. Both the beast and his false prophet were thrown alive into the lake of*

fire that burns with sulfur. Their entire army was killed by the sharp sword that came out of the mouth of the one riding on the white horse. And all the vultures of the sky gorged themselves on the dead bodies.

Jesus and the saints will return back to this earth on horseback. I always wondered why Jesus doesn't return to fight the battle of Armageddon in a spaceship from outer space—you know, like those futuristic outer space movies try to make us all believe that the world's last battle will be fought in outer space. I was praying about this, and I just came out and asked the Lord myself. *"Why are you returning riding on top of a horse out in the open where you would be vulnerable? Why not in a spaceship or a military tank like our military uses or in a fighter jet?"* Then the Lord answered me very quickly. He said, *"The Battle of Armageddon is not going to be fought in outer space or in the sky, so I won't need a spaceship or a jet fighter. The battle is on the ground and even, so I won't need an armored tank. The battle will be won with the Sword of the Spirit, which is my Word, and my Word is sufficient. I also happen to love horses."*

The time is now to choose which side that you want to be on. I've given you Scripture from the end of the Bible. Jesus and the Christians win. The Word of God also says in Joshua 24:15 *"Choose you this day who you will serve."* You can make that choice right now; it must be made now while you're still in the land of the living. Once you die, it's too late. Those who have accepted Jesus of Nazareth as Lord of their lives before the rapture will not be judged. We are exempt saved from having to go through that process because our sins have been forgiven. Then all will see with their own eyes that Jesus is indeed the true King of Kings and the only way the true God.

Oh, and that proverbial white picket fence of indecision that some of you have been sitting on—it doesn't even exist. It's another one of the devil's lies. You see unbeknownst to you, if you haven't chosen Jesus as your King and Savior now, you've already been shoved into the devil's group who will drop dead at the end of the tribulation from the glory of our coming Lord and Savior Jesus Christ. At the end of the thousand year reign of Jesus Christ they will be raised again from the dead to receive their condemnation and eternal judgment. You've been shoved into the devil's group who will be raised to life again for their condemnation on judgment day. There is no middle ground. There are only two sides: God's side or the devil's side. You must make your choice now before you die. The faith that Jehovah God gave to all of us along with His Word will help you to receive Jesus Christ's free gift of everlasting life. The Bible says in Hebrews 10:38, "*The just shall live by faith.*"

All this is done here before you die. There are no second chances. This is not a game of chance. This is a decision between you and Jesus. Just tell Him this prayer out loud. The Holy Spirit and all of heaven are listening. I guarantee you have their attention. The greatest miracle is **the miracle of salvation**:

> *Lord Jesus Christ of Nazareth, I accept you as my King and savior. I repent for my sins, please forgive me for them now. Thank You for paying that high price for me and washing me as clean as the driven snow. I give you my life now. Please fix it and teach me the right way to live. In Jesus Christ of Nazareth's name I pray, amen.*

The Beginning!

Book Summary

In this groundbreaking book called *Breaking the Chains of Spiritual Bondage between Man and God's Creatures*, you will be shocked and amazed as I take you through the Word of God to reveal once and for all just where Sasquatch, the skunk ape, and yeti came from and what they really are!

With the Word of God, I will reveal to you the doors that the Lord has been showing me that demons use to come in and steal and kill from us. Demons also use a person's lack of wisdom in the Word of God to lead them astray. Also I will show you how your own manmade traditions are used as a door by devils to waltz right into your life and steal from you.

The laws of sowing and reaping play a gigantic part with you and your animals. Sowing a high quality of life into the animals you own determines whether you will be more or less prosperous. There are hundreds of other areas in your life you don't know about where demons come in and steal from you. I'm not talking about all those other areas right now. I'm only talking about the areas concerning the way you take care of the animals that God has put in front of your eyes and the animals that are in your ownership.

This book will help you to make the right choices for your animal's wellbeing and yours. I warn you, take care of the animals that Jehovah God has put into your life.

Now you will be equipped with the biblical wisdom in this book to shut those doors and push those thieving devils right out of your finances and life forever.

AUTHOR BIOGRAPHY

Rebecca is the older of two girls the other is her sister Robin Christie Sundberg. Both women call San Diego California their home. The Holy Spirit first fell all over Rebecca and put this heavy burden on her for the animals of this world when she was walking down a warm sidewalk in El Paso Texas at the tender age of five. He talked to her about the wrong treatment of the animals of this earth and let her feel His pain for them. It was in 1999 when the Holy Spirit moved Rebecca to put everything that He had been showing her for the past fifty years into this explosive and revealing book. This is Jehovah God's thoughts on how He wants us to all care for the animals in each of our lives. So, here it is, I pray that you enjoy it!